C000185724

FOUL DEEDS & SUSPICIOUS
DEATHS IN EALING

FOUL DEEDS AND SUSPICIOUS DEATHS Series

Wharncliffe's *Foul Deeds and Suspicious Deaths* series explores, in detail, crimes of passion, brutal murders and foul misdemeanours from early modern times to the present day. Victorian street crime, mysterious deaths and modern murders tell tales where passion, jealousy and social deprivation brought unexpected violence to those involved. From unexplained death and suicide to murder and manslaughter, the books provide a fascinating insight into the lives of both victims and perpetrators as well as society as a whole.

Other titles in the series include:

Foul Deeds and Suspicious Deaths in Bolton, Glynis Cooper
ISBN: 1-903425-63-8. £9.99

Foul Deeds and Suspicious Deaths in London's East End, Geoffrey Howse
ISBN: 1-903425-71-9. £10.99

Foul Deeds and Suspicious Deaths in & around Durham, Maureen Anderson
ISBN: 1-903425-46-8. £9.99

Foul Deeds and Suspicious Deaths in Hampstead, Holburn & St Pancras, Mark Aston
ISBN: 1-903425-94-8. £10.99

Foul Deeds and Suspicious Deaths in Colchester, Patrick Denney
ISBN: 1-903425-80-8. £10.99

Foul Deeds and Suspicious Deaths in Newport, Terry Underwood
ISBN: 1-903425-59-X. £9.99

Foul Deeds and Suspicious Deaths Around Derby, Kevin Turton
ISBN: 1-903425-76-X. £9.99

Foul Deeds and Suspicious Deaths in and Around Scunthorpe, Stephen Wade
ISBN: 1-903425-88-3. £9.99

More Foul Deeds and Suspicious Deaths in Wakefield, Kate Taylor
ISBN: 1-903425-48-4. £9.99

Foul Deeds and Suspicious Deaths in York, Keith Henson
ISBN: 1-903425-33-6. £9.99

Foul Deeds and Suspicious Deaths on the Yorkshire Coast, Alan Whitworth
ISBN: 1-903425-01-8. £9.99

Foul Deeds and Suspicious Deaths in Coventry, David McGrory
ISBN: 1-903425-57-3. £9.99

Foul Deeds and Suspicious Deaths in Manchester, Martin Baggoley
ISBN: 1-903425-65-4. £9.99

Foul Deeds and Suspicious Deaths in Newcastle, Maureen Anderson
ISBN: 1-903425-34-4. £9.99

Foul Deeds and Suspicious Deaths in Hull, David Goodman
ISBN: 1-903425-43-3. £9.99

Foul Deeds and Suspicious Deaths Around Newport, Terry Underwood
ISBN: 1-903425-59-X. £9.99

Please contact us via any of the methods below for more information or a catalogue.
WHARNCLIFFE BOOKS
47 Church Street – Barnsley – South Yorkshire S70 2AS
Tel: 01226 734555 – 734222; Fax: 01226 724438
E-mail: enquiries@pen-and-sword.co.uk
Website: www.wharncliffebooks.co.uk

Foul Deeds & Suspicious Deaths in

EALING

JONATHAN OATES

Series Editor
Brian Elliott

Wharncliffe Books

First Published in Great Britain in 2006 by
Wharncliffe Books
an imprint of
Pen and Sword Books Ltd
47 Church Street
Barnsley
South Yorkshire
S70 2AS

Copyright © Jonathan Oates 2006

ISBN: 1 845630 12 2
ISBN: 978 1 845630 12 6

The right of Jonathan Oates to be identified as the Author
of this Work has been asserted by him in accordance with
the Copyright, Designs and Patents Act 1988.

A CIP catalogue record for this book is available from the
British Library.

All rights reserved. No part of this publication may be
reproduced, stored in a retrieval system, or transmitted, in
any form or by any means, electronic, mechanical,
photocopying, recording or otherwise, without the prior
permission in writing of the publishers.

Typeset in 10/12pt Plantin by Concept, Huddersfield.

Printed and bound in England by CPI UK.

Pen and Sword Books Ltd incorporates the Imprints of
Pen & Sword Aviation, Pen & Sword Maritime,
Pen & Sword Military, Wharncliffe Books,
Pen & Sword Select, Pen and Sword Military Classics
and Leo Cooper.

For a complete list of Pen & Sword titles please contact
PEN & SWORD BOOKS LIMITED
47 Church Street
Barnsley
South Yorkshire
S70 2BR
England
E-mail: enquiries@pen-and-sword.co.uk
Website: www.pen-and-sword.co.uk

Contents

Acknowledgements

I wish to thank Mr Paul Fitzmaurice, Mr William Bignell and Mr John Gauss for reading the text and for making many helpful suggestions and comments.

The historic pictures reproduced here are courtesy of the London Borough of Ealing and from the postcard collection of Mr Reginald Eden (a member of the West London Postcard Club).

Finally, I would like to thank my wife for her encouragement and for taking the contemporary photographs which appear in the book.

I dedicate this book to my inlaws, Mr and Mrs William Bignell.

Preface

There have been many books published about Ealing's history, dating from Faulkner's *Antiquities of Brentford, Ealing and Chiswick* in 1845, Jackson's *History of Ealing* in 1898, to the more recent *Ealing and Hanwell Past* by Peter Hounsell and Eileen Reid's *Brentham, 1901–2001*. Yet the earlier ones are antiquarian in tone and the latter are in the great liberal tradition, where social and economic progress are the predominant themes. Those written by Charles Jones at the turn of the twentieth century, *Ealing: From Village to Corporate Town* and *Ealing: A Decade of Progress*, written as they were by a major local public dignitary, trumpeted Ealing's civic achievements in a most obvious manner, as did Scouse's *Ealing, 1901–1951*. No hint of crime appeared in these works, though, to be fair, there had been relatively few murders in Ealing. It is true that the public events of the terrible seventeenth century – civil war and plague – usually have their place as reminders of the bad old days, but generally these narratives give the impression of peaceful progress and a lack of criminal activity. What is missing, to use the words of Sherlock Holmes in *A Study in Scarlet*, is 'the scarlet thread of murder running through the colourless skein of life'.

Books about real life crime in Britain abound, including those which focus on murder in London and its environs. Yet these surveys are necessarily limited in scope and only a very few of the murders related here have appeared in book form, notably, the murders of Spencer Perceval and William Terriss, the Chesney killings, and, rather less well known, the killings of Arthur Wheeler and the Crockers.

The purpose of this book is to investigate serious crimes and untimely deaths in and around Ealing from the fifteenth century, when they were first recorded, to the Chesney killings of 1954. The cut-off date chosen is arbitrary; but to proceed up to more recent years would be unwise. First, because they are too recent and too many people who are directly involved are still alive. Secondly, because there have been so many that one would have to be highly selective. Killers who were apprehended in Ealing, such as William Corder of the Red Barn Murder, but whose misdeeds were committed elsewhere, are excluded.

My definition of Ealing is the current London Borough of Ealing, formed in 1965, which includes Acton, Greenford, Northolt, Perivale, Southall, and Hanwell. Also included is Brentford, which, until 1863, was part of the old parish of Ealing, which stretched south to the Thames. Not all the murders occur within these boundaries. Unlawful deaths of Ealing residents which occurred elsewhere are also included – the best known being the slaying of Spencer Perceval and that of William Terriss.

My aim is not to show that previous historians writing about Ealing have covered up a dark and criminal past in a favour of emphasizing the respectability of the 'Queen of the Suburbs'. Serious crime in Ealing was low – in the centuries under investigation, there were forty-nine murders plus several infanticides, though space does not allow them all to be chronicled here. Compared to more recent years, this is a scanty tally indeed (from 1972 to 1987 there were at least thirty-nine). This is not to argue that the past was a golden age where crime in Ealing was rare. It was not. Lesser crime was common – horses were beaten, wives abused, there were con men, assaults, burglaries, drunkenness and begging cases, all of which cropped up frequently in the local police courts. Yet murder was very unusual.

I have tried to maintain a degree of anonymity over the domestic residences where murders were committed, by only naming the road or street where they occurred, not the exact location. Their identity can be easily verified, though, should anyone wish to do so. Public buildings associated with murder, such as Ealing Town Hall and various public houses, are, of course, exempt from such a ruling.

Tracking down the murders of the past is a little like detective work itself. Since so little has been written about crime in Ealing, published books are of limited use, except to highlight the well known cases of Perceval, Chesney and Terriss. There were four main overlapping sources of information, none of which in itself was complete. First, for the sixteenth and seventeenth centuries, the calendars of Middlesex Quarter Session Rolls were invaluable. Secondly, the Old Bailey website provided details of crimes from 1678 to 1834. Then there are the newspapers, both local and national. From the nineteenth century onwards, lengthy reporting of the discovery of crime, inquests and trials appeared in the press. If there was not a trial, less information was forthcoming. As Sherlock Holmes rightly remarked, 'The press, Watson, is a valuable institution, if only you know how to use it'. *The Times* Digital Archive, covering 1785–1985, has been of great use, but it is not comprehensive – for instance, the Crocker killings are not recorded at all – but it does point the investigator towards a number of murders he may have missed altogether. The indexes to the *Acton Gazette* for 1871–1965 are also useful. Finally, there are the Metropolitan Police murder and manslaughter registers, which cover 1891–1954. These are the most comprehensive list, but even they omit one or two crimes, and for the period *c.* 1917–27, locations are excluded in the register, making it next to impossible to discover where these took place (this is one reason why this book does not contain many murders from this period). The registers make it possible to check murder files, which contain the complete statements from suspects, witnesses, police and other officials. It is a pity that Ealing's three diarists of the 1930s to 1950s did not make any comments about any of the murders.

This book is aimed both at those interested in crime and those interested in local history. Before the meat of the matter begins, there are chapters which set the scene for what is to follow. The first is a summary of the general local history of Ealing and its environs. The second concerns the sinews of law and order; chiefly the police (and their forerunners)

Eille Norwood (an Ealing resident) as Sherlock Holmes, c. 1920. The author

and the courts, both local and in London, whose responsibility it was to deal with the crime and disorder detailed in subsequent chapters. Then there are the chapters detailing the murders themselves, in chronological order, except for a chapter of three short cases of infanticide, which have been pulled together. Not all concern murder. Some are of public events, such as the burning of the Marian martyrs. Others concern treason or crimes for which the death penalty existed and was used at that time.

This book emerged from a talk the author gave about crime in Ealing in April 2005. There is, naturally, some overlap between the two, but there is much here which was not in that talk. As to his qualifications for the present work, the author has had a number of books published on the local history of the districts in question, as well as articles published in the journal of the Sherlock Holmes Society of London. He is, though, no criminologist. However, by a freak of fate, he did live (unknowingly) for three years next to a house in which one of the double murders chronicled here occurred.

CHAPTER 1

Ealing and its Environs – a Brief Outline

Ealing is unquestionably a delightful place to live in.

Ealing was one of many villages, and small towns, in the county of Middlesex. Until around 1870, the county was largely rural, despite its proximity to the ever expanding metropolis of Empire. Some of these villages, such as Ealing, Acton, Brentford and Hanwell, were linked by the main roads leading westwards from the capital. Acton was 5 miles from London, Ealing seven and Hanwell eight. In the case of all these villages, that road was the Oxford, later the Uxbridge, Road. The Great West Road ran through Brentford, a Thames-side town.

Ealing's origins are obscure. There was no Roman settlement here; it is thought that it was originally a Saxon village in the seventh century, although it was not recorded as an individual entity in Domesday. In the Middle Ages, these villages were small farming communities, centred around the parish church and more or less run by the manorial system. Ealing, Acton and Brentford were part of the manor of Fulham, which was held by the Bishop of London from the King. Generally speaking, little is known about the origins and early history of these places, due to the lack of both documentary and archaeological evidence, but this need not trouble us too much because most of this book concerns the post-Reformation era, for which there is far more evidence.

The manorial system fell into a slow decline from the sixteenth century and the parish began to emerge as the principal unit of local government. Each parish was a semi-independent part of the county, running its own affairs, but overseen by the Middlesex Quarter Sessions, which was an administrative as well as a judicial body, which will be referred to again in the next chapter. The vestry ran parish affairs, collecting rates to pay for the care of the local poor, to repair the roads and bridges and to maintain the church.

These villages had very small populations; mostly only in the hundreds until the late eighteenth century. In 1599, Ealing's residents

Pitzhanger Manor, Ealing, c.1939. Reg Eden's collection

only numbered 426. Population growth was very slow until the later
nineteenth century. Daniel Defoe only referred to one of these
villages, Brentford, when writing his famous *Tour around the Whole
Island of Great Britain*, published in the mid-1720s. However, as with
many villages around London, they became home to minor courtiers,
gentlemen and retired merchants. Shakespeare's son in law, John
Hall, lived in Acton in the seventeenth century, as did one of
Cromwell's generals, Philip Skippon.

By the eighteenth century, we have a better idea of how these
villages looked. Inns flourished along the main roads. In Ealing there
was *The Bell, The Green Man, The Feathers* and *The Old Hats*. Hanwell
had *The Coach and Horses*, and Acton's oldest hostelries were *The
King's Head* and *The George and Dragon*. As well as being useful for
locals to meet, drink and gossip, they were important for travellers
along the main road and for the stage-coach horses to be rested and
changed. By 1826, there were a dozen inns in Ealing. Most of Ealing's
houses were centred around the church, the Uxbridge Road and
scattered in the hamlets of Little Ealing to the south and Ealing Dean
to the west.

Schools began to be founded, often by charitable bequests in the
wills of local residents. Lady Anne Rawlinson's will was proved in
1714 and provided for small schools for poor children in Ealing. In
1786, a Sunday school was opened and taught 160 pupils in 1826.

Private education had existed here since at least 1599, and in about 1698, the Great Ealing School is thought to have begun its long and illustrious existence. There were other private schools, both boarding and preparatory, catering for girls as well as boys.

Ealing became known as a place of royal residences in the late eighteenth century. Princess Amelia, George II's favourite daughter, chose Gunnersbury House in 1761 as her summer residence – convenient for Kew, London and Windsor. Later, Edward Augustus, Duke of Kent, George III's son, bought a house in north Ealing in order to install Madame St Laurent, his French Canadian mistress. Later the Duke married and his daughter was to become Queen Victoria.

Although most of the people in these parishes were Anglicans and so attended the parish churches, there were pockets of religious dissent in the seventeenth century. Richard Baxter had formed a Nonconformist conventicle in Acton, and another famous Dissenter, John Owen, lived in Ealing. Catholics were even fewer in number. These were minorities. For most of the population, the Anglican clergyman, who usually lived in the parish by the eighteenth century, was a significant figure of authority.

Village Ealing of 1826 possessed 'many handsome residences in and around the parish'. It was home to at least 33 gentry and clergy. Serving their immediate needs were a variety of shops. There were butchers, bakers, general dealers and wheelwrights. There was also the medical practice of Dickinson and Hutchinson, surgeons. Mail arrived at 8.00 in the morning, being dispatched at the same time and then at 3.00 in the afternoon from Ellen Lawrence's post office on Ealing Common.

The development of Ealing and its environs was, after the mid-seventeenth century, peaceful. There were no outbreaks of rebellion or riots here. Save for a few fights between navvies and locals in the 1830s and the invasion scares of the Napoleonic era which led to the founding of local volunteer forces, it was as tranquil a place as any in England.

The pattern of life began to change slowly. The Grand Junction Canal had already been dug through Middlesex, through the parishes of Southall, Greenford and Perivale, at the end of the eighteenth century, linking the industrial Midlands with London. This gave a spur to the local economy as agricultural produce could be more easily brought to London whilst rubbish came westwards, much of it to be used as manure.

It was the Great Western Railway, however, which had the greatest long-term impact. In 1838, trains began to run from Paddington westwards, and there were stations at Ealing and Hanwell in 1838, and at Southall in 1839. This stimulated a little extra building, but not much. Carriages, horse buses and stage-coaches were probably far more prevalent than the trains until later in the century, when train services were improved and trains on the District Line began to serve Ealing.

The Victorian age was an age of change. In the 1820s, Ealing was unquestionably a village; by the 1890s she was a rapidly expanding town. Charles Jones, borough surveyor from 1863 to 1913 was a key agent in this. Public amenities, such as lighting, drainage, sewage, and the preservation of some land as public parks, all fell under his remit. In 1901 borough status was achieved, Ealing being the first borough in Middlesex. More contentious was the tram issue, but in the same year, the London United Electric Tram Co. began to run trams from Shepherd's Bush to Southall, through Ealing and Acton. Department stores, such as Saunders and Sayers, appeared to serve a rather more sophisticated clientele. Churches blossomed in the later nineteenth century; in 1850 there was one Anglican church – in 1900 there were nine, as well as six Nonconformist and two Catholic chapels.

It was largely a middle class society. For the latter half of the nineteenth century, its leading light was Spencer Walpole, MP, and three times Home Secretary, of the Hall, Ealing Green. He was the president of numerous social clubs and did much to encourage them. The political clubs in the district were mostly Conservative. Council-funded schools were avoided until 1903. A cottage hospital, founded in 1869, was maintained by voluntary subscriptions. Small private schools were numerous. That said, there were significant pockets of the working class in West Ealing and South Ealing, where Ealing's first council houses were built in 1899.

At the turn of the twentieth century, Ealing was perhaps at the zenith of its social fame. It was known, from about 1904, as the Queen of the Suburbs, an epithet which is still occasionally in use a century later, though the term was first used to describe Richmond. In 1912, Ealing was described thus:

> *Ealing is unquestionably a delightful place to live in. The borough has an area of 3,225 acres: has been laid out in a very pleasant fashion, and possesses all the qualifications which appeal to the business man who has been in 'populous city pent' and is desirous of spending his money and leisure hours away from 'London's roar'.*

Further attractions of Ealing were low rates, low death rates, 'some of the smartest and attractive shops and business establishments outside London', and good transport links to and from London. The local

Ealing Railway Station (District Line), c.1900. Reg Eden's collection

theatre, the Lyric, which was patronized by the unfortunate Sarah Higgs and her friends in the 1890s (see chapter 16), was said to 'be the centre of social life in Ealing'. Open spaces had been preserved from the builder, including Walpole Park, where the public library was located, Ealing Common and Lammas Park. The stereotypical resident was the retired officer from the Indian Army or Indian Civil Service.

Nearby Acton grew considerably in these years, too, but was more working class and industrial in character. Its chief industry was the laundries – over 200 existed in 1900, earning it the title of 'Soapsud Island'. Other industries included Napiers, the car manufacturers, and Wilkinson's Sword Co. Southall also grew in this period into an industrial zone, with the Danish Margarine factory employing several thousands, while Hanwell, squeezed between Southall and Ealing, was more of a suburb, like Ealing, with little industry. The northern parishes of Greenford, Northolt and Perivale remained small farming communities.

After the First World War, the borough of Ealing expanded, bringing the adjacent parishes of Northolt, Perivale, Greenford and Hanwell under its jurisdiction. It became a parliamentary borough in 1918, and always elected a Conservative member in this period.

Ealing Common, c.1931. Reg Eden's collection

Whilst Ealing itself remained a commuter suburb, the northern districts of Greenford and Perivale became the location for industries such as the Rockware Glass Works, Lyons, Glaxo and the Hoover factory, all of which benefited from the building of the Western Avenue in the 1930s. These once rural northern parishes rapidly lost their former character as rows of terraced and semi-detached houses were built.

Sporting and other societies flourished. Golfing and tennis were the two main sports which were well catered for in Ealing. There were seven golf courses in or near the borough. There were tennis courts, both grass and hard, in the public parks as well as numerous private ones. One tennis coach who was to gain notoriety in 1936 was Linford Derrick (see chapter 23). In 1928 Questor's Theatre was founded and became a leading amateur dramatic club.

By this time, Ealing, Acton and other adjacent places had become part of the suburbs of western London and they had lost something of the sense of being independent entities. From a population of nearly 70,000 in 1921, the enlarged borough of Ealing had grown to 116,771 ten years later.

Although over 300 Ealing residents were killed by German bombing in the Second World War, and several prominent buildings, along with hundreds of houses, were destroyed, the district was less badly

Ealing Broadway

(COPYRIGHT)   "WAKEFIELD" SERIES, EALING, W."
No. 110

Ealing Broadway, c.1910. Reg Eden's collection

affected than many in London. Building continued in the only corner of the borough which was still rural – Northolt – with Labour and Conservative governments trying to outbid each other in the number of council houses they could erect in order to deal with the housing shortage. It was here that Jean Cull's young life was tragically ended in 1952 (see chapter 29). At this time, the borough's population was about 187,200. It had largely become part of the western suburban sprawl. Politically, the district was changing, too, with Arthur Hudson being Ealing's first Labour MP in 1945. It was also in the immediate post-war years that Ealing became nationally and internationally known, with the production of the films known as the Ealing Comedies, at the Ealing Film Studios. With its excellent transport links and numerous open spaces it was still a pleasant place to live.

Ealing Studios, 1953. LBE

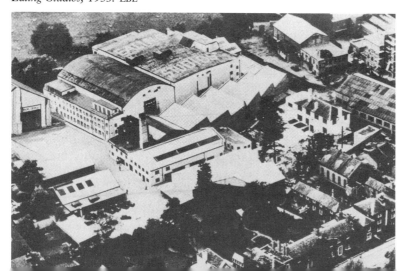

Chapter 2

The Framework of Law and Order

The system of Police would be 'obnoxious, a tyrannic system of espionage, subversion of the liberties of Englishmen'.

Before moving on to crimes in Ealing, it is necessary to survey the forces operating on the side of justice in the period under consideration; namely from the Middle Ages until the 1950s. Police, courts and punishment will be now under scrutiny, especially as regards Ealing and its environs.

In the Middle Ages, the sheriff, or the shire reeve, was the officer responsible to the King for the administration of justice, among other duties, in each English county. The methods at his disposal were primitive, as he had no permanent force with which to enforce royal justice. Instead, he had to rely on the men of the county coming to his or his deputies' aid in time of crisis in order to apprehend evildoers. From 1361, the justices of the peace were instituted in order to deal with offences. JPs were gentlemen, but many lacked legal knowledge.

In the sixteenth century, changes made by the Tudor monarchs had an enormous impact on the system of justice. The role of the sheriff fell into decline and the JPs became the real rulers of the county. They convened four times each year in full session, but could also deal with minor offenders individually or in small numbers. However, they did not try crimes which merited the death penalty. These included not only murder and treason, but also the theft of items valued at 12*d* or over (many items stolen were deliberately undervalued) and other offences, the number rising sharply in the eighteenth century. Forgery and highway robbery were also capital offences in this period.

As well as the JPs, the parish constables were an important part of the system of justice. Constables had existed as manorial officers in the Middle Ages, but by the sixteenth century, they, as well as the JPs, had a greater role. Each parish had to select one or two men to serve, unpaid (except for expenses, such as beer money and travel costs) for a year as constable. No training was given and no prior experience was deemed necessary. These men had to help in the capture of criminals and in taking them to the JPs to be examined. The constables have often been portrayed as bumbling amateurs, comic figures and all but useless, but this is too simple a picture. Many were men of substance locally; their knowledge of their parish was intimate and so they were often able to achieve results. The fictional Dogberry in Shakespeare's *Much Ado About Nothing* is a figure of fun, but it is he who arrests the criminal.

Once suspects had been brought before the JPs, they could then be sent to prison, if the JPs thought there was a genuine case against them. Prisons were there in order to secure suspects prior to trial – they were not for detaining them as a form of punishment. The prison which served the Middlesex parishes as well as London was the ancient prison of Newgate, which was rebuilt in 1782 after it had burnt to the ground during the Gordon Riots of 1780. Noblemen were held in the Tower of London and debtors in the Fleet.

Serious offences in England were brought before the county Assizes, which were held twice a year. Unlike other counties, though, there were no Assize courts held in Middlesex. Instead, prisoners were tried for capital offences at the Central Criminal Court (the official name for the Old Bailey), before a judge and jury. There would usually be a counsel for the Crown and one for the prisoner. The Old Bailey held sessions once a month. The Middlesex prisoner, at least, did not have to spend a long time in prison before his fate would be decided.

The ultimate penalty for crime was the death penalty. Executions were by hanging (beheading was a privilege of noble traitors) and, until 1783, took place in public at Tyburn, on the corner of Hyde Park. These attracted great crowds – Dr Dodd's allegedly had 500,000 spectators. They were in public in order that the condemned man or woman made a final confession and acknowledged their guilt before society. Afterwards, executions took place outside Newgate. In 1868, they took place in private – in the prison where the guilty person was held (Newgate until its demolition in 1902). Most of the crimes which had been punishable by death had the capital sentence removed from them in the 1820s. Murder and treason were the two exceptions. Capital punishment for murder was modified in 1957 and was abolished outright in 1965.

Other punishments included transportation to the American colonies from the seventeenth and eighteenth centuries. After American independence, Australia was used as a destination for prisoners being transported. With the abolition of this system in 1868, penal servitude was substituted. This meant that the prisoner had to suffer imprisonment with hard labour. This was abolished in 1948. Gaol sentences were another form of punishment, but were rarely given to convicted murderers. Those guilty of the lesser offence of manslaughter (where a killing is not premeditated) were usually gaoled.

Some cases involved suspects whose mental condition was such that questions were raised over their responsibility for their actions. From 1843 until 1957, the courts relied on the McNaghten Rules as a test of a suspect's responsibility for his crime. Doctors, acting for the Crown, had to show that a suspect was incapable of knowing right from wrong. Men and women who were saved from the rope because of this were sent, after 1860, to the Broadmoor Criminal Lunatic Asylum in Berkshire (later named the Broadmoor Institution). If the mental condition of inmates improved, they could be released, as free men (or women).

The other important agent in the judicial system was the coroner, who, with a jury, had to investigate any suspicious death. Usually they would assemble in a nearby public house (or other public building, such as a town hall) to examine the corpse, whose identity would be verified by their next of kin, hear medical details from a local doctor (or police surgeon) and listen to the testimonies of any witnesses. They then had to decide the cause of death and who was responsible – whether a named individual or person or persons unknown. It was only then that the case could proceed to trial, via a local court before reaching the Old Bailey. From the later nineteenth century Ealing cases were heard at Brentford Police Court until 1919, when the Ealing Police Court was first used.

Circumstantial evidence has generally had a bad press, but it is on this that most criminals are found guilty. It is anything but eyewitness testimony, which leads to a conviction. It usually takes the form of an accumulation of evidence which leads the jury to find a suspect guilty. The opinion of the jury is based on the evidence which has been presented to them during a trial.

This system of justice remained basically the same from the sixteenth century to the 1960s. It was far from perfect and all too human failings were evident throughout. One example was in 1828 when Dr Bond, a schoolmaster and JP of Hanwell, suspected his servant girl of theft. He had her imprisoned in the parish lock up during freezing weather. Two days later, with only beer from the constable and a blanket from her fellow servants, she was found to be suffering from the cold. Bond then released her. A report in *The Times* concluded that he had abused his powers, as he lacked the authority

Fordhook; Ealing, 1903, briefly residence of Henry Fielding. LBE

to let her go and had not completed any of the relevant paperwork. He came in for a stiff reprimand and for public embarrassment.

However, the detection of crime changed considerably from the sixteenth to the twentieth century. The role of the parish constable has already been alluded to. In London and its environs, there were other methods. In 1753, Henry Fielding (briefly a resident of Ealing in 1753–4), novelist, journalist and JP, along with his half-brother, John, formed the Bow Street Runners. These men have often been seen as the forerunners of the police force, but care needs to be taken here. This was a very small force of men, operating both on horseback and on foot. However, they were salaried, unlike the constables in the parishes or the 'thief takers', men who caught criminals for rewards. They were also permanent. Under the supervision of the energetic Fielding brothers, they had some successes in breaking up gangs of criminals. Yet some of their members were as corrupt as the criminals and in any case, they were too few in number to have a great impact throughout the capital and its surroundings.

Apart from the constables and the Bow Street Runners, there were other measures taken to combat crime. In Hanwell in 1821 an association was formed of the prominent men of the parish, each man pledging to pay for rewards in order to encourage others to catch local criminals. It is not known how successful this was.

The major changes in policing occurred after 1829. In this year, a highly controversial Act had been passed by the reforming Home Secretary, Sir Robert Peel. Based on his experience in dealing with crime in Ireland, he created the Metropolitan Police Force. The force covered London (excepting the City of London, which had its own force) and soon afterwards spread to cover Middlesex and the fringes of Kent, Essex and Surrey. The Met's area of jurisdiction of nearly 700 square miles was divided into twenty-two districts, each headed by a superintendent. Ealing, Hanwell and Acton all fell under the Metropolitan District X. The Met's headquarters was at Great Scotland Yard until 1890, and at New Scotland Yard on the Victoria Embankment thereafter.

Many feared that the police, or Peelers as they were known, would be government spies and that the liberties of the people would be suppressed as they were on the Continent. It was not only Radicals and criminals who feared the police. In Ealing in 1830 a resolution was passed by the ratepayers which was highly critical of this new system. They concluded that the police would be 'obnoxious, a tyrannic system of espionage, [and] subversive of the liberties of Englishmen'. Because there had been so few burglaries in Ealing in the previous decade, the police rate of £880 annually was far more than the £100 on average lost per year in thefts.

It is not certain when Ealing first had a resident policeman. None are recorded in the directories for the 1830s, but there is a reference to the payment of the police rate in the vestry minutes of 1838. According to the 1841 census, the police station was on Ealing High Street and was manned (there were very few women police until the second half of the twentieth century and none in Victorian times) by a sergeant, John Pasco, aged about 32. Working with him were about six constables. As the population increased, so did the police force. In 1878, George Wells is noted as being the police inspector for the parish. Smaller parishes, such as Hanwell and Greenford, had a sergeant throughout the late nineteenth century.

Different systems of law enforcement ran in tandem during the nineteenth century. Parish constables were still appointed, but the post became less onerous as the nineteenth century progressed and was eventually abolished. The Bow Street Runners existed in tandem with the Metropolitan Force for some years, before the two were amalgamated.

The police were uniformed in blue and carried truncheons. They could be issued with cutlasses if the need arose, and inspectors could

Policemen at Ealing Police Station, c.1904. LBE

carry pistols. They were under the control of the police commissioner, who was answerable to the Home Secretary. This resulted in local control being lost. The new force had many imperfections, such as corruption and, above all, drunkenness. There were also allegations of brutality. A policeman was found guilty of theft from *The Green Man*, Ealing. However, the visible police presence helped to prevent crime as well as apprehend criminals. It also resulted in a degree of uniformity, order and control. There was still hostility to the police in the Victorian era – leading to the shooting of PC Davey in Acton in 1863 (see chapter 14).

Apart from the regular uniformed police, there was also from 1842 the Detective Department. Until 1878, this plain-clothed body of men was very small in number and their duties overlapped with their uniformed colleagues. Thereafter, it was they who had the responsibility to investigate murder. They were assisted by the development of forensic science. As time progressed, more scientific methods were employed. Fingerprint identification methods were used from 1901 and Home Office analysts were employed to discover pertinent infor-

High Street, Ealing.

Police Station, Ealing High Street, c.1910. LBE

mation about the cause of death in murder cases. One leading expert was Sir Bernard Spilsbury (1877–1947) who became somewhat of a celebrity, being involved in the Crippen case in 1912, as well as a number chronicled in this book.

Over the years, as Ealing's population increased, so did the police presence. Proper police stations were built. By the end of the nineteenth century, the police were seen as a useful force of men in the suppression of crime and disorder. They were of use in the General Strike in 1926. When Alexander Goodlett, an Ealing resident, was attacked by youths in Ealing in 1934, he could record that two officers promptly came to the scene of the crime and gave the miscreants a good telling off. A policeman gave the young Jack Cull some fatherly advice in 1952, though this did not have particularly successful results (see chapter 29).

Criminals faced the full barrage of the forces of law and order: first, in being identified and secondly in being punished for their crimes. Yet, though the law was not always effective and some murders remained unsolved, it usually brought miscreants to justice.

Chapter 3

Medieval Treason
1443

Cause them to be hanged thereupon ... cast down upon the ground when half dead, their heads to be struck off, their bowells to be burned ...

Very little is known of any criminal activity in this locality prior to the sixteenth century because of the lack of surviving evidence. Even where information exists, the amount concerning any particular incident is extremely scanty, unless members of the nobility or Church were involved. A couple of references to criminal assault in this district in this period include the wounding of John Braynt in Southall in 1382 when seven men attacked him and inflicted sword cuts to his person. Sir Simon Rede, brother of the chaplain of St Mary's Church Acton, killed one of the King's enemies on the highway in 1458, but was subsequently pardoned.

The reign of Henry VI (1422–61) was a troubled one. Abroad, the Hundred Years War with France continued until its disastrous end in 1453. At home, the King, who succeeded his father Henry V, as a baby, was unsuited for the rough trade of kingship in the Middle Ages. Although open rebellion did not break out until 1450 and civil war in 1455, troubles began before then. Law and order was breaking down.

On 13 May 1443, there was an order for the sheriffs of London to meet the marshal of the King's Prison of Marshalsea on London Bridge. The law officers were to bring with them their prisoners. These included four Ealing men: John Botelier, a painter, Robert Baister, a baker, John William, a chaplain, and Thomas Homade, a scrivener. According to the order in question, these men were, 'all lately in the King's court convicted of divers treasons', and because of this the sheriffs had to ensure that the following was their fate:

> *to the gallows of Tyburn, and to cause them to be hanged thereupon . . .*
> *cast down upon the ground when half dead, their heads to be struck off,*

Richard Amondesham and family, fifteenth-century Ealing residents. LBE

*their bowells to be burned, the body of every one of them to be quartered,
and their heads to be set upon the bridge.*

What exactly this treason was is unstated. Treason is the crime of
conspiring against the state. Presumably these men were plotting
against the King, but why and how are other questions. Were they
part of a wider plan, perhaps in conjunction with Richard Duke of
York, who was to make war on Henry VI in 1455, or were they
religious radicals? It is impossible to know and forms a grisly
beginning to the Ealing experience of dark deeds and untimely deaths.

Chapter 4

The Brentford Martyrs 1558

Fires flaming about them, they yielded their souls, bodies, and lives, unto the hands of the omnipotent Lord.

On 14 July 1558, six men suffered an agonizing death by fire in Brentford. The flames in which they perished were not an accident. The men were burnt deliberately by fires ignited by human hands. Why had this happened?

People had been burnt for their beliefs since the late Middle Ages in both Britain and Europe because they held religious views which were not in accordance with those of the Catholic Church. These men and women were known to the church courts as heretics and their offence was heresy. Because religion and politics were inseparable, rulers were usually happy to uphold authority in all its forms. Since the Protestant Reformation of the early sixteenth century, Catholic rulers were firm in their mission to stamp out this new form of what they termed heresy.

In England, following Henry VIII's break with Rome, his son's government made moves to replace Catholicism with the new religion. However, with Edward VI's death in 1553, his sister, Mary, came to the throne. She was a devout Catholic and was determined to return England to the Catholic fold.

Part of her policy was to act directly against the heretics. Starting with the senior clergy who had pushed forward the Reformation, including the Archbishop of Canterbury, Cranmer, and Bishops Latimer and Ridley, Protestants were arrested and if they did not recant, were, from 1555, burnt at the stake.

The Reformation had gained a foothold in and around London. In 1558, six men were arrested in the village of Islington, just north of the capital. These men were Robert Milles, Stephen Cotton, Robert Dynes, Stephen Wright, John Slade and William Pikes. We know very little about any of these men, except that Pikes was a tanner from Ipswich. They were probably all very ordinary craftsmen and workers, unlikely to form much of a threat to the emerging status quo.

It cannot be said that the legal process by which the men were convicted was unduly harsh and they were given every opportunity to avoid their ultimate and dreadful fate. Thomas Darbyshire, Chancellor to Edmund Bonner, Bishop of London, called them before him at separate times; Milles on 20 June, Wright on the following day, then Cotton and Slade, then Dynes and Pikes on 23 June. Darbyshire went through the same articles with each man, whom he saw separately. Had they attended mass recently or received the sacraments of the Catholic Church? Milles and Wright had not been since 1557; Slade and Pikes since 1553, Cotton since 1552 and Dynes had last attended mass in 1551.

To compound their offences in the eyes of Darbyshire and his masters, the six added that they thought the rites, customs and ceremonies of the Roman Church were all against God's word, so they refused to observe and keep the same. Milles and Wight had not received the sacrament since 1557. Milles said he would not attend church whilst there was a cross and religious images (which appeared to some Protestants as idolatry) there. Slade agreed. They also claimed that Catholicism was in opposition to God's word. They thought that Latin should not be used in services because it could not be understood by the majority of the congregation. Finally, they all agreed that they would only take the sacrament if it was the same as it had been under the Protestant Edward VI.

These were not the answers the Queen's servants wished to hear. All six were summoned to appear before Darbyshire on 11 July at St Paul's Cathedral. He asked them to turn from their beliefs and return to the Catholic fold. If they refused, they were to tell him if there was any reason why they should not be condemned as heretics, 'whereupon they all answered, that they would not go from the truth, nor relent from any part of the same while they lived'.

On the afternoon of the next day the six men had another meeting with the bishop's chancellor. It was then that they heard the sentence to be passed upon them. According to George Foxe, chronicler of the Marian martyrs, 'the said chancellor condemned those poor lambs, and delivered them over to the secular power, who received and carried them to prison immediately and kept them in safety, till the day of their death'. Darbyshire, on the same day as he passed sentence on them, wrote a certificate for the Lord Chancellor, which led to a writ being produced on 13 July, which was the order that the men be sent to Brentford and there to burn.

It is not stated why the men were sent to Brentford – none of them were native to the town. It may have been selected as it was close to the capital and so convenient for such punishment. It may also have been chosen because it was a market town where a numerous crowd might be expected to gather and to learn the fate of heretics, and thus benefit from the example.

When they arrived at Brentford, on the following day, the men remained resolute, and were taken to the Butts. The chronicler wrote of their deaths thus:

> *Whereunto they being brought, made their humble prayers unto the Lord Jesus, undressed themselves, went joyfully to the stake (whereunto they were bound), and the fires flaming about them, they yielded their souls, bodies, and lives, unto the hands of the omnipotent Lord, for whose cause they did suffer, and to whose protection I commend thee.*

Their deaths were particularly painful, not out of any intended cruelty, but because their executioners were relatively unskilled at their job. Gunpowder was often used in such burnings on the Continent so that men died relatively easier. But some saw in the deaths a kind of victory. It was said that one of the burning martyrs desired God to send a token of recognition, so that those watching the spectacle might know that they died for the right cause. Therefore, a white cross, as broad as a man's hand, was apparently seen on the man's breast, from shoulder to shoulder.

Almost four months after the deaths of the six men in Brentford, the childless Mary died. Her victims had not died in vain, for their deaths indicated that the Protestant faith was not restricted to a

The Butts, Brentford, 2005. The author

handful of powerful men whose motives for adopting the new religion were materialistic. It had extended throughout all ranks of society and, for some, was so strong that they would and did die for their religious beliefs. Approximately 300 did so in a matter of only three years. Contrary to one of Shakespeare's dictums ('Conscience doth make cowards of us all'), conscience had made them courageous. Although the number of total deaths was tiny by European standards, it was not by those of England and created a powerful propaganda message for the disseminators of Protestantism in England for the following centuries and enabled Mary to be branded with the un-enviable soubriquet 'Bloody'.

Chapter 5

The First Murder
1588

John Prior took an axe to
the head of one Agnes East.

T he year 1588 is rightly remembered as the year in which the invasion attempt of the Spanish Armada was defeated. More locally, it was the year in which the first known murder was committed. This took place in Hanwell. Unfortunately, very little is known about it. There were no newspapers to describe it and court records are scanty, partly due to the killer's ultimate fate.

What happened was this. On 15 January 1588, between 8 and 9 o'clock in the evening, one John Prior took an axe to the head of one Agnes East. The victim died at once. This murder was committed in 'the Hall', which was the house of one Thomas Millett, presumably a local gentleman. Prior fled immediately and once abroad was free

St Mary's Church, Hanwell, c.1750. LBE

from the forces of the law. A coroner's inquisition was held on the following day, but no more was done. Agnes's body was buried in the churchyard on 21 January.

Who were the people involved? The parish registers do not begin until 1570 and so we do not know if either was local. The victim may have been the Agnes East who was born in Chesham in Buckinghamshire on 29 January 1575. She may have been a servant girl employed at the Hall. Prior may have been a fellow servant or he may have been a thief who broke into the Hall for the purpose of theft and was interrupted by the unfortunate Agnes. We do not even know where the Hall was.

A sad, sordid and brief episode with which to begin this chronology of Ealing murders.

Chapter 6

Found Innocent of Murder, Found Guilty of Theft
1716

At the stile to the field they found a man leaning upon it. He was covered in blood.

ohn Sweetbones was born in Acton in about 1695 and was apprenticed to a bricklayer, but he also seems to have been a hardened criminal, a burglar, thief and murderer. In 1717 he was indicted at the Old Bailey for three offences. At first, his luck had held. On 8 April 1716, he is said to have broken into William Trafford's house and stolen a shirt and a waistcoat. He was found not guilty. But his more significant crime was on 22 December of that year.

Thomas Peacock, at about 6.00 in the evening, recorded that he heard a man moaning in a nearby field. He thought that this must be someone in distress. Cautiously, he decided that he should seek help from his neighbours before investigating the matter. None would accompany him. The moaning could still be heard, but the voice was growing weaker and weaker. Peacock armed himself with his pitch-fork and a lantern and finally persuaded another man to come with him.

At the stile to the field they found a man leaning upon it. He was covered in blood. On closer inspection, his pockets had been turned inside out and he appeared to have been dragged along the ground. However, with his last dregs of energy, he had managed to reach the stile. The man was one John Mims. Peacock and his neighbour dragged him home, but not before he fainted. On being asked who his attacker was, Mims had been unable to answer. He had been hit on the left side of his head with a hammer, and the wound was a quarter of an inch deep. He died two days later.

Peacock recalled that he had seen Mims earlier on 22 December and that he had been wearing a hat. No hat had been found at the scene of the crime or nearby. But he later saw it on Christopher

Acton fields and village, 1700s. LBE

Barnel's head. Barnel explained that he had bought it from Elizabeth Lewis. She said that she had found the hat thrown into the cellar of Elizabeth Alloway. Finally, Elizabeth Alloway said that one John Sweetbones had thrown it 'down there out of Roguery'. After further investigation a Mr Prince related how Sweetbones left Prince's lodgings in St Giles in London, on 21 December, saying he was going to Acton to see his mother, and that he returned at 8.00 on the following day, the day of the murder.

Elizabeth Lewis reported that, on 21 December, Sweetbones had no money and so she lent him 6*d*. By the evening of the following day, his material circumstances had changed for the better. So much so that he asked Mrs Prince, his landlady, how much he owed her. Sweetbones gave her a guinea to change, and then he gave her between 16 and 17*s* out of that. He alleged that his mother had given him this money. Further circumstantial evidence against him was that the sleeve of his frock was almost torn off and his hands were bloody. However, Sweetbones claimed this was because he had been fighting with a friend in St James' Haymarket. This friend could not be produced as a witness, because he was said to be a soldier who had left with his regiment for Scotland.

Then there was the matter of the hat. As to how he had two hats, he said that one belonged to his friend. One Mr Cheesebrook backed him up on this point. Yet Mary Beal, the granddaughter of the deceased, said that her grandfather's key was the one found on Sweetbones. In his defence, he said that it was his and that he had owned it for five years.

Sweetbones tried to enlist in the army on 16 January 1717, but when it was known that a murder charge hung above him, he was told to join up at once. Sweetbones said he would not, as he was innocent and had nothing to fear. Sweetbones was correct, at least, initially. When he was tried for murder at the Old Bailey on 27 February 1717, he was acquitted. But he was not yet a free man. There was the little business of robbing Mims of a hat, valued at 7*s*, and a key valued at 1*s*. 'He was a Third time indicted for Robbing John Mims'.

Here the evidence was more conclusive. Thomas Ogaleshaw, a hatter, said that he had sold the hat to Mims, and had seen him wearing it shortly before the murder. The witnesses who had previously made statements about the fate of the hat after it had left Mims's possession repeated them. The key that was alleged to belong to Mims was used on the lock of Mims's chest and was found to open it. Sweetbones's mother could not swear that she had given him any money, though his sister said that she had told her that she had. Sweetbones 'not being able to prove any one thing he had said, nor say any thing but what he had said upon the last Indictment, the Jury found him guilty of This'. Since the items were valued at over 12*d*, this constituted grand larceny and the penalty was death. John Sweetbones was hanged shortly after.

Chapter 7

Three Cases of Infanticide
1721, 1740 and 1899

That she not having God before her Eyes ... did make an assault ...

In the early modern world, contraceptives were almost unknown, which meant that sex outside marriage was relatively uncommon. When it did happen, and when babies appeared, there were several possible courses of action. The usual ones were to marry the father (where known, and assuming he was not already married) or to raise the child as a bastard, with financial help from either the father or the parish. But there was a more drastic solution – murder – either directly or by simple neglect, such as leaving the baby in a field on a cold winter's night, to die of exposure, and none being the wiser as to its parentage. Three cases follow where babies died and the supposition was that they had been murdered.

Pleasant Roberts (1721)
Ralph Norris was called on by Katherine Davis and Eleanor Moseley in the summer of 1721. The women had been searching a cess pool with a poker and 'felt something, but could not come at it'. He brought some tongs with him and lifted up to the bottom with them. What he found was the corpse of a new-born infant.

Pleasant Roberts, a single woman of Hanwell, was accused of murdering her male bastard son by throwing it into a cess pool and was tried before the Old Bailey on 30 August 1721. A witness, one Abigail Partridge, said that the child was much bruised about the head, that the skin from the left side was damaged and that the baby was of full growth. Katharine Davis agreed with this statement, adding that the baby's nose had bled. Eleanor Moseley recalled that Pleasant Roberts seemed unwell at supper on the day before the discovery, but had put it down to sour beer, not the last stage of pregnancy.

Pleasant Roberts said in her defence that she had given birth at about midnight, but that the child was stillborn. She then disposed of it as has been mentioned. Yet she had been planning to care for it, had it been born live. At her sister's house was a trunk to which she had the key, and when this was unlocked by Richard Greene, a friend of Pleasant's brother, they found children's linen. This was produced in court in order to verify Pleasant's remarks. Another witness, William Tate, said that he had seen Greene take the linen from the chest in order to produce in court. Other parishioners swore to Pleasant's good character. Finally, 'The Jury considering the whole matter, Acquitted her'.

Elizabeth Evans (1740)

A similar case from this neighbourhood came before the same court two decades later. Elizabeth Evans of Ealing was accused of having brought a bastard female child into the world, 'that she not having God before her Eyes ... did make an assault ... with both her hands' on the baby, killing it by choking and strangulation with the aid of a linen handkerchief.

Sophia Claxton was the first witness and she said that Elizabeth, who shared the same bed with her, had complained of a pain in her limbs and stayed in bed for three days. After a hard day's work, Sophia returned home and went to bed. She saw Elizabeth get up in the middle of the night and was apparently going to the cess pool to relieve herself. Next morning, Sophia went to work, but before she did, she put the bedclothes back on the bed to cover Elizabeth. Then she saw, underneath her gown, a large handkerchief. In this handkerchief was a baby. On asking Elizabeth why she did not call for help and what she had been doing, she received no reply. Sophia could not recall whether the baby was stillborn, nor whether it was bruised. Also Elizabeth would not say whether it was her own. Sophia was extremely puzzled why her bedfellow had not confided in her.

Elizabeth Holman was a midwife and, although not present at the point of birth, had arrived shortly afterwards. The child was fully grown, but was dead when she saw it. She was unsure whether it had been born alive or not. She did not notice any mark on the body. She asked the mother how she came to kill it. The mother replied that she did not kill it but found it dead. She said that before she would have killed it, she would have gone begging with it. As to the father's identity, she could not say. It could have been any one of three men, all of whom lived outside the parish – one lived 30 miles away.

Elizabeth Evans's character was sworn to by Elizabeth Pearce, her landlady. She said that the accused had lived in her house for a year and a half, 'and I never saw any Harm by her in my Life'. She did not know that she was pregnant until Sophia told her. 'I asked her, how she came to be so naughty? And she made no Answer at all.' There

St Mary's Church, Ealing, 1740. LBE

were no other witnesses to call in her defence and she could only state that she did not kill her baby. Fortunately, the jury agreed with her version of events, and acquitted her.

Both of these women had been lucky in so far as they were not found guilty of murder, though courts were usually lenient. They were probably innocent. Many babies of women at all levels of society were dead when they were delivered and so the fate of those of Pleasant Roberts and Elizabeth Evans was unsurprising.

Person or Persons Unknown (1899)

On the morning of Wednesday, 19 April 1899, Mrs Louisa Mason of Troy Farm, Brentford, was walking to work along Bollo Lane, Acton. She worked at Mill Hill Park Laundry, but just before she reached her place of work, she noticed something odd when passing the garden of Edward Cheeseman, which was close to the laundry. There was a black bag under a tree near to the railings. She bent down on her knees, put her hand through the railings, opened the bag and pulled out what appeared to be a white calico nightgown.

Whilst Louisa was wondering about what to do, Eliza Fisher, who also worked at the laundry, approached her. Louisa then told her that she believed that there was a baby inside the bag, on account of what she had seen so far. She then went to Mr Cheeseman's house and told him what she had found. On his way to fetch the police, he met PC William Stuckey on his beat. When the two men returned, they found that a small crowd had gathered around the tragic bundle. By this time, Louisa had left the scene in order to start work.

On the following day, there was an inquest at the council offices. Detective Wood noted that the bag was of American black cloth, which could be bought for 3 or 4*d*. The body was wrapped in brown paper and wore a red twill petticoat, with the letters A and Z and the figures 9 and 15 written on them. There were no marks

Bollo Lane, Acton, 2005. The author

of identification whatsoever. Dr Lingham had examined the tiny body and he had discovered that the decomposing corpse's lungs had been fully inflated and that the piece of tape tied tightly around its neck had been the cause of death. The baby had been born between a month and six weeks before. Although the verdict of wilful murder against person or persons unknown was brought, the identity of the killer was, and remained, unknown. The most likely suspect would have been the anonymous mother.

The coroner concluded,

> *a number of bodies of unknown children were found in this neighbour-hood. This may be accounted for by the fact that when girls got into trouble the first step they took was to find work in a laundry, such employment being easily obtained when they could do nothing else.*

The coroner's officer added 'there were a great many laundries in Acton, and this probably accounted for the large number of girls here'. Four years later, a Brentford girl working in the Acton laundries killed her baby.

How often this type of killing was in Acton is unknown; but it appears, by the coroner's remarks, that it was a common tragedy, and one of its times. Presumably the mother was a laundry girl and disposed of the child in the district in which she worked.

From 1922, infanticide was treated as manslaughter instead of murder, as hitherto had been the case. In any event, before then, most women tried for killing their new born babies were reprieved.

Chapter 8

Friends Falling Out
1725

For God's sake,
run for a Surgeon.

iolent death is usually the action of someone known to the victim, rather than of a complete stranger. Friendships can turn ugly and the following is a tragic example. Robert Cook of Hanwell and George Merrick of Southall were two gentlemen, who, on 11 February 1725, went to *The Red Lion Inn*, Brentford High Street, and there met three army officers. They drank and talked in one of the inn's upper rooms. Although the evening began in good spirits, it had a bloody conclusion.

At about 11.00 at night, the three soldiers left the inn. Cook and Merrick ordered a bowl of punch and 'appeared very pleasant and friendly'. About an hour later, the two men decided to play a game and called for dice. After a servant had brought these to them, he departed, and then heard a noise only 5 minutes later. He ran upstairs to find out what was happening.

He must have been taken aback by what he saw. The two men who had, until a few minutes ago, been the best of friends, were facing each other, swords drawn. Cook was backed up against a wall and so could retreat no further. The servant ran downstairs in order to fetch help. When they returned, the two men were on the floor, Cook being uppermost. On disentangling them, it was evident that both had been wounded, and Merrick seriously so.

Cook called his former adversary 'his dear Merrick' and, turning to a servant, said 'For God's sake, run for a Surgeon'. James Bethune, a surgeon, was contacted soon enough, but he needed time in order to assemble his tools and other necessary items. During this interlude, Merrick and Cook conversed. This was their dialogue:

Merrick: *Dear Cook, was it you that did it?*
Cook: *Dear Merrick, it was.*
Merrick: *I freely forgive you.*
Cook: *But was it not your seeking?*

Site of The Red Lion, *Brentford High Street,* 2005. The author

There was no response from Merrick. He was laid on a bed by a servant and the latter asked the injured man how he was. Merrick said that he felt well and enquired after Cook. When Bethune finally arrived, at about 2.00 in the morning, Cook, who was wounded in two places, had 'bled pretty much', but insisted that Merrick be attended to first. Bethune later said that he found the two gentlemen 'standing together in a friendly manner'. While Merrick was being treated, Cook fainted, but he would not allow his wounds be seen to before those of his friend.

Merrick's wounds were, indeed, very serious. He had lost over a pint of blood and the opinion of another surgeon was thought necessary. One Mr Holloway was sent for. He and Bethune perceived that Cook's sword had pierced right through Merrick's body. At this point, Cook interjected with a question, 'Merrick, you Know 'twas your own Fault?' This question received no answer. Meanwhile the surgeons opened Merrick's body and found that the sword had 'perforated the cavity of the Belly, and wounded the Guts in two places'. Merrick died at 11.00 in the evening of 12 February.

The trial came before the Old Bailey on 24 February. Cook, who was accused of murder, said that Merrick had drawn his sword and then stood between him and the door, forcing him to draw his own weapon in self-defence. The soldiers who had been in their company earlier in the evening and the inn's servants swore that there had been no prior quarrel between the two men. Indeed, Cook had asked one of them to remain with them when the three were talking about leaving – hardly evidence of him wanting to commit a murder and then asking for a witness to be present. Several noblemen, such as the Duke of Richmond and the Earl of Essex, gave testimony to Cook's good character, that he was a peaceful man and not one prone to quarrels.

Others would have made similar comments, but the court did not believe further evidence was needed.

The verdict of self-defence was brought and so Cook walked away as a free man. What we shall never know is why Merrick decided to threaten his friend's life. It can only have been in a flicker of madness, brought on by alcohol, as the two seemed very solicitous for each other after the fatal encounter had taken place. Merrick had plenty of time to incriminate Cook in front of witnesses had it been Cook who had attempted to kill him.

Chapter 9

Murder on the Highway
1747

Great Enquiry is making after the villains to bring them to Justice.

nyone acquainted with the London newspapers in 1747 would have been aware that murder, assault and theft on the roads around London were at a serious level. A few of these thieves were gentlemanly – one, having robbed a man on 1 January 1747, then wished him a very happy new year. Most were not so polite and what happened in Ealing in 1747 was just one of those cases. However, not for the first or last time, the initial reporting of this incident, although correct in broad outline, was wrong in detail.

At least two London newspapers carried exactly the same story at the end of January 1747. According to them, on the evening of Saturday 24 January, a farmer and his son, who lived at *The Old Hats Inn*, West Ealing, 2 miles from Acton on the Oxford Road, were on their way back from London, presumably where they had been on business. They stopped at Acton for a pint of beer. On finishing their drink, the father left immediately, while the son remained to pay the bill. A quarter of a mile along the road, the farmer was attacked by two men.

Hearing sounds of a struggle, his son ran to his father's rescue, accompanied by fellow drinkers. When they arrived, they found his father injured, but still breathing. He had been shot twice and one bullet was in his left breast. On the morning of 26 January, he died. According to the newspapers 'great Enquiry is making [sic] after the villains to bring them to Justice'.

In contrast, a couple of days later, *The General Advertiser*, another London newspaper, made the following remark, 'The Affair of the Farmer shot near Ealing, having been misrepresented in several of the Papers, had occasioned our publishing the Facts at large, which we have had from his Neighbours'. What happened was this. Samuel Verry 'an honest, substantial Farmer of Oxendon-hill [presumably

The Feathers Inn, *Ealing, c.1860.* LBE

Horsenden Hill], in the Parish of Perivale, Middlesex' was going home on 24 January at 7.00 in the evening, accompanied by John Thomas Verry, his 17-year-old son. Leaving the main road from London, they travelled northwards towards Perivale along Castle Bear (now Castlebar) Road. This was a lonely stretch of road, with very few habitations.

They went by an empty house which had been that of Dr Holling, where they passed two men loitering in the road. Verry senior rode straight past them, clearly having caught the two by surprise. They then tried to stop his son's progress, but he escaped them and rode back to the inn called The Sign of the Feathers (since 1998 imaginatively renamed The Town House) and shouted 'Murder'.

Verry looked back towards his son, but was prevented from riding back to him by one of the robbers, who proceeded to attempt to rob the farmer. Verry was 'somewhat in liquor and a stout man', and struck the would-be thief 'a Violent Blow'. His companion in crime then shot Verry and robbed him of some of his money. Despite this, the wounded man managed to ride back to the inn where he met his son and some other men who were coming to his assistance. It was too late to do anything about the thieves and the whole party returned to the inn.

Although he had been wounded, Verry 'thought himself not much Hurt: And he seemed very Hearty'. Even so, he was bleeding heavily. Once back at the inn, he was seated, stripped of his clothes and a surgeon was sent for. The doctor found a bullet in his left breast, which he removed. Verry remained conscious throughout, and 'settled his affairs'; presumably by making a will. Finally he gave a warning, based on his recent experience, saying that he 'earnestly desired all people to be cautious of travelling late, or making Resistance if attacked by such Villains'. This advice is still appropriate over two and a half centuries later. He died at 2 o'clock on Monday morning, 26 January, and was buried in the churchyard of St Mary's Perivale.

Two days after his death, Noah and William Groves were examined by James Clitheroe of Boston House, a local JP. The two had been seen loading pistols on the evening of the attack. On 30 January the two men were gaoled on suspicion of murder.

About one month later is the last reference concerning this matter. It was known that the King, George II, had offered a pardon to anyone who could reveal the identity of the killer of Samuel Verry, except the guilty man himself. This indicates that the Groves brothers were probably released prior to even being tried. This could have been because of the lack of evidence against them, or the fact that they had

St Mary's Church, Perivale, c.1900. Reg Eden's collection

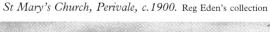

alibis for the time in question. In any case, there was only one witness, Verry's son, and he may not have been able to recognize the two as the men who killed his father as at best he would only have had time to have caught a glimpse at them on a dark winter evening. This supposition is strengthened by the fact that Verry's friends and relations offered the sum of £30 to anyone who could bring his killer to justice.

Unfortunately, nothing more is known of this matter. The newspapers do not refer to anyone being caught or tried for this crime at the next two sessions of the Old Bailey in February and April 1747, and nor do the records of cases held before the Old Bailey, either. Yet another unsolved murder to darken the annals of crime.

Chapter 10

The Last Robbery of John Rann
1774

I know no more of the affair what these gentlemen, that belongs to Sir John, that wants to do things to swear my life away.

In 1774, according to Horace Walpole, cultured man of letters, England was undergoing somewhat of a crime wave. He wrote on 6 October of that year thus:

Our roads are so infested by highwaymen, that it is dangerous stirring out almost by day. Lady Hertford was attacked on Hounslow Heath at 3.00 in the afternoon. Dr Eliot was shot at three days ago without having resisted, and the day before yesterday, we were near losing our Prime Minister Lord North; the robber shot at the postilion and wounded the latter. In short, all the freebooters, that are not in London, have taken to the highway.

Yet Walpole did have a sense of the dramatic. The forces of law and order were not wholly useless in their efforts to apprehend highwaymen. The robber who met Lord North and took his watch and money was apprehended two days later, for instance. It is worth noting that this theft took place on Gunnersbury Lane, Ealing. This seems to have been a favoured place for highwaymen.

A better documented case of highway robbery on Gunnersbury Lane in 1774 is that involving Dr William Bell and John Rann on 26 September. It is odd that Walpole did not mention this incident, because he was a regular visitor to Gunnersbury House, summer residence of Princess Amelia, aunt of George III. Dr Bell (1731–1816) was the Princess's chaplain and was to become a distinguished theologian and a noted benefactor.

John Rann, alias 'Sixteen String Jack', was a rather different character. He was born in about 1750, possibly in a village near Bath. He began his working life as a servant in Bath, graduating to being a

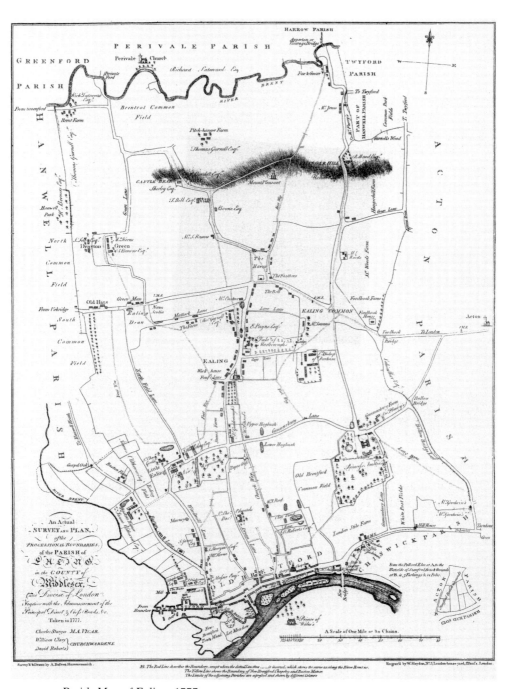

Parish Map of Ealing, 1777. LBE

coachman for the Earl of Sandwich. Exactly why and when he turned to crime is unknown, but he first attracted the notice of the law in November 1773, when, as part of a gang, he was arrested on suspicion of having taken part in a stage-coach robbery at Hampstead. Fortunately for Rann and his associates, neither the coachman nor the passengers could identify them as the criminals. Despite this, he remained a highwayman, and managed to be acquitted on another two occasions at the Old Bailey in April and May 1774.

Rann was at the height of his short-lived fame – a far cry from his humble origins – in the summer of 1774. He had acquired a mistress, who was also one of his accomplices, one Eleanor Roache. They attended race meetings, Rann being conspicuously dressed. He wore a scarlet coat, tambour waistcoat, silk stockings, laced hat and other finery. Being naturally handsome also helped. He acquired his nickname from the eight silk ribbons which hung from each knee of his breeches.

All this was to change. Dr Bell was riding to Gunnersbury House, presumably from London, and had reached Gunnersbury Lane at just after 3.15 in the afternoon of Monday 26 September 1774. He saw two men on horse-back, slowly riding one behind the other, just in front of him. Something seemed odd to the clergyman. He took out his glass and, putting it to his eye, saw that one of the men's hats had its flaps down and a red handkerchief was attached to it. Thinking their 'dress and appearance being somewhat singular' he wondered who they were. He claimed not to have had the slightest concern that they were highwaymen. In any case, their slow speed allowed him to pass them by, just as they were leaving the few houses on the road.

Bell noticed that one man wore a light coloured coat, a hat flapping around his head and long black hair and rode a brown horse. This man looked sallow and sickly in appearance. The second man wore a frock coat, buttoned up, and rode a black horse. He seemed rather healthier than his companion. Both looked back at Bell, who returned from his inspection of them and briefly thought of them no more.

Bell turned towards Gunnersbury and his destination. However, Bell could soon hear the sounds of two horses riding towards him. Thinking he could also hear carriage wheels, Bell looked out again to see what other traffic was on the road. He could see none, but assumed that it was in the hollow in the road immediately behind him. A little later, he could hear two horses again, but knowing that they were not pulling any form of transport, knew he did not need to get out of the way.

Yet when the two horsemen drew neck and neck with him, Bell realized that they were the men whom he had earlier passed. He still did not think they were highwaymen. One ordered Bell to stop and Bell reined in his horse. The man demanded 'Your Money'. Bell answered with a question 'My Money?' The man was in no mood for such answers and replied 'Yes, or I will blow your brains out'. He then reached inside his coat as if to draw a pistol, but did not do so. Bell certainly hesitated no longer and said 'I will give it you'. He gave the man his money, 18*d* in all (not a great deal of money, even then), but the latter, seeing the doctor's rather more valuable silver watch, demanded that, too. Bell was then told to ride on, which he did. The two thieves galloped away.

It looked as if Rann and his friend had been successful. They returned to London with their ill-gotten gains. Rann had his mistress and her servant, Christian Stewart, take the watch to a pawnbrokers to obtain cash. They went to John Cordy's shop on Berwick Street that very evening. Although only Cordy's lad was at the shop, he fetched his master and asked them if it was their watch. They said it belonged to a gentleman. Cordy refused and said he could not lend any money on it unless its owner was there in person. This annoyed them, but they could do little. Cordy knew where the two lived and, after they had gone, he went to Sir John Fielding.

The half-blind Sir John Fielding, known as 'the Blind Beak', was a London magistrate and a co-founder of the Bow Street Runners. He sent two of his men, Blanchville Clarke and William Halliburton, with Cordy and they searched Eleanor Roache's lodgings, arriving there

Gunnersbury House, Ealing, 1797. LBE

at ten. There they found two wet and dirty boots which had been worn recently. They also visited the man who made the watch and he told them it was Dr Bell's. The two women, and their companions, John Rann and William Collier, were arrested and brought before Fielding.

Two days later, Bell went to Bow Street in order to try and identify his assailants. He hoped he would be able to do so because the two men had not disguised their faces when they robbed him. However, once in court, he could make no instant recognition. 'I could not have sworn to them, there was so much differ-ence, though at the same time so much likeness'. He looked at them again and again. He became certain that Rann was the man who robbed him, though was less sure of Collier, who had stood – assuming it was

Princess Amelia, c.1770. LBE

indeed he – behind him when the robbery had taken place.

The four were tried at the Old Bailey on 19 October for highway robbery and for receiving stolen goods. Dr Bell was the principal witness and he gave his story to the assembled court. He was questioned over the identity of the man who robbed him and he reaffirmed this was Rann, and he was also pretty certain that Collier had been his accomplice. John Cordy testified, and Bell confirmed, that the watch he had been offered by Eleanor Roache was indeed Bell's.

This evidence was backed up by one William Hill, a servant of Princess Amelia. He reported having seen Rann and another man, identity unknown, in Acton that afternoon. He also noticed that their boots were dirty. The constables who made the search and arrests also related their stories, as did Eleanor Roache's landlady, Hannah Craggs. Matters looked black for Rann and his associates.

Rann made the following defence:

> *I know no more of it than a child does unborn, nor I never seed Mr Bell before he came to Sir John's, which Mr Bell must be certain of, for to think for me, for to come to him on the middle of the day, for to rob him,*

which I was never guilty of; I know no more of the affair what these gentlemen, that belongs to Sir John, that wants to do things to swear my life away, for I don't know what.

He went on to say that Eleanor would easily swear his life away and the other witnesses were lying. Eleanor denied that Rann had given her the watch.

The court found Rann and Collier guilty, sentencing them to death, but recommending mercy for Collier. Eleanor Roache was transported for 14 years and her servant was acquitted.

Rann was executed at Tyburn on 30 November, dressed in a bright pea green coat and with an immense favour in the button hole – a celebrity to the last. He would have been pleased, had he but known it, that two years later, Dr Samuel Johnson, remarked 'Sixteen string Jack towered above the common mark'. Yet there seems to be little to mourn in the passing of this flamboyant and (temporarily) lucky criminal. It is, in any case, unlikely that Johnson would have celebrated a live and dangerous miscreant.

Chapter 11

The Impecunious Parson
1777

I am sure my Lord Chesterfield don't want my life.

Our previous miscreant was from the lower ranks of the Georgian social order. Our next came from a rather more privileged background. His connection with Ealing is perhaps tenuous, but it seems too notable a tale to be excluded. The Revd Dr William Dodd had been born in 1729, the eldest son of a parson. He attended Clare College, Cambridge, between 1746 and 1749 and embarked on a literary career, though he was also a schoolmaster and a clergyman.

This sounds like a recipe for success. But it was also the germ of his downfall. After marriage in 1751 and initial literary achievements, he leased an expensive house in Wardour Street, London. Dodd's chief difficulty throughout life was that his financial means were inadequate to meet his outgoings, which were far from frugal. It is an old story, and Dodd resorted to a number of expedients in order to square the circle. To begin with, these were all legitimate.

Having been ordained in holy orders, he took posts as a clergyman in West Ham and lectureships in churches in the City. Money from his wife led him to opening a chapel behind Buckingham House (later Palace) in the hope of attracting royalty and nobility. He was appointed as a royal chaplain, but the venture did not succeed, nor did his works of literature and he was sacked from an editorship of a journal. He did not receive any of the clerical posts he had sought. He also founded a small private school for boys in Ealing, on Pope's Lane, in 1765. One of his most socially prominent pupils was Philip Dormer Stanhope, Earl of Chesterfield. The school, like his other ventures, failed, and it closed in 1771, once Chesterfield left to go on the Grand Tour. It is possible the school folded because of Chesterfield's departure. Yet the young nobleman's part in Dodd's life was not over.

Dodd was not an unlikable character. He worked hard and was involved in a number of charities. He helped to found a charity to help those imprisoned for small debts, the Royal Humane Society and the Magdalen Hospital in order to reform prostitutes. Having been robbed by a highwayman, Dodd tried to intercede for the man's life after the death sentence was passed. But Dodd also tried to ingratiate himself with the world of the aristocracy, keeping a carriage and dressing fashionably, which caused some to accuse him of vanity and pomposity. Perhaps the observer who summed him up the best was one who referred to his good temper, but also his want of prudence.

In the 1770s matters looked bleak. Creditors became more pressing and his sources of income dried up. Attempts at bribery by his wife on his behalf led him to be struck off the list of royal clergy. His popularity as a preacher also faded. However, there was some revival in Dodd's fortunes as Chesterfield managed to find him a clergyman's post in Berkshire and he took up writing again.

The beginning of the final act began in February 1777. According to *The Gentleman's Magazine*, 'The Doctor, being pressed for money to pay his tradesmen's bills for the year past, had recourse to this desperate expedient to support his credit'. It also revealed that Dodd had another string to his bow – that of forgery. He forged a bond, and signed it with the name of his former pupil, Chesterfield, who had now just turned 21. A bond was similar to a cheque in that it could be presented at a bank and cashed, provided that the person whose signature was on it had money at the bank in question.

This bond was made out for £4,200, and one Lewis Robertson, a broker, was employed by Dodd to arrange the transaction at Henry Fletcher's bank in the City. On 4 February Robertson did so. Fletcher's assistant, Samuel Peach, did not notice anything suspicious at first, and gave the £4,200 to Robertson, who accordingly took it to Dodd. The bond was passed on to Fletcher's attorney, one Mr Mansley.

Mansley examined the bond and his suspicions were aroused by a blot on the date, claiming later 'it struck him as something singular'. There were also a number of scratches near the blot. Mansley alerted Fletcher and the two of them called on Chesterfield so that he could prepare another bond which would be correct in all particulars. On 7 February they spoke with Chesterfield and it was then that the forgery was discovered. Chesterfield had not signed a bond for that amount on that day.

The investigation then began. Once the Lord Mayor was alerted, Dodd and Robertson were summoned to appear before the magistrates. Dodd denied nothing, though he was 'very much shocked' and claimed that 'urgent necessity had pressed him to it'. He had meant no injury to Chesterfield and would repay him as soon as possible. He pleaded for mercy and that he not be prosecuted. His unwitting accomplice, Robertson, said that he had believed that the bond was that of Chesterfield and he believed that Dodd was acting on the behalf of his former pupil. Robertson was discharged, having been found innocent.

Dodd was tried on 19 February at the Old Bailey, it being resolved that he

> feloniously did falsely make, forge, and counterfeit . . . a certain paper writing . . . purporting to be a bond, and to be signed by the Rt. Hon. The Earl of Chesterfield.

The noble lord was called to speak for the prosecution. He said that the signature was not his, and, having known Dodd for many years, could recognize Dodd's handwriting on the bond. Other witnesses examined the bond and swore that it was not Chesterfield's writing, but Dodd's. Dodd was told that if he could return all the money he would be discharged, but he could not, as £300 had already been used to pay his creditors. He confessed that he had done wrong, but begged for mercy, saying

> Lord Chesterfield cannot but have some tenderness for me as my pupil; I love him and he knows it. There is nobody who wishes to prosecute. I am sure my Lord Chesterfield don't want my life; I hope he will shew clemency to me. Mercy should triumph over justice.

When asked why the bond was not made for only the £300 he urgently needed to pay his bills, he remarked that it would have looked suspicious for a nobleman to make out a bond for so small an amount, whereas a larger sum was far more probable.

The jury only took 10 minutes to decide that he was guilty, but put in a plea for mercy. Forgery was then a capital charge, so Dodd faced death if he did not win a reprieve or a royal pardon. There were many who were ready and willing to plead his cause. Horace Walpole wrote 'I own I felt very much for the poor wretch's protracted sufferings'. Dr Johnson, who thought Dodd should have been transported, wrote to the King and the Lord Chancellor on his behalf, and there were petitions from the City, the two universities and elsewhere to try and save his life. Newspapers which had once scorned him now wrote favourably about his plight.

It was thought by *The Morning Advertiser* that the King and his Council would have granted a pardon, 'had they not been apprehensive of the most fatal consequences arising in this commercial kingdom, as the natural consequence of forgery'. Yet, though Dodd was brought before the Bench again on 14 May, it was all to no avail.

St Lawrence's Church, Cowley, 2005. The author

He was a condemned man and would suffer. When his friends visited him, they tried to console him that he was leaving a 'wretched world' to enter a better one. Dodd disagreed, arguing that he liked the present world very much, if he only could have lived in it rather longer.

On 27 June 1777, Dodd was led out to Tyburn. Allegedly, half a million turned out to line his route. He addressed his audience 'God bless ye all',

> *which words were uttered with so moving and unaffected an emphasis, as to draw tears, apparently, from eyes unused to weep; men, women and children, of all ranks were observed to weep; a genuine evidence of gentle hearts and unutterable anguish.*

Johnson wrote 'He died with pious composure and resolution'. After he was hanged, his body was taken to St Lawrence's Cowley, in Middlesex, where his brother was the vicar and a plaque was put up to commemorate his life, virtues and chief concerns.

Dodd was the last man in England to be executed for forgery; a claim to fame which, of course, he never sought.

Chapter 12

Murder of a Prime Minister 1812

He could not have shot a greater rascal.

As every schoolboy was once supposed to know, the one thing Spencer Perceval is remembered for is that he is the only British Prime Minister to have been successfully assassinated (to date), compared to four American Presidents. There have been attempts to kill other premiers – such as Sir Robert Peel in 1843, Margaret Thatcher in 1984 and John Major in 1991 – but all have failed. As a contemporary chronicle put it, this was 'one of those atrocious events, which, to the honour of the British Nation, rarely occurs'. The murder of Perceval is certainly the best-known crime in this book, but what is usually overlooked is his connection with Ealing.

Spencer Perceval was born in 1762, attended Harrow and Christ Church College, Oxford. On leaving university he became a lawyer and then entered Parliament as a Tory MP. By the first decade of the nineteenth century he was a rising star of the government, first as Attorney-General and then as Chancellor of the Exchequer. He supported the abolition of the slave trade and restrictions on child labour, but not parliamentary reform or Catholic Emancipation. In 1809 he became Prime Minister and served for another three years. In this period his government did their best to prosecute the war against Napoleonic France.

In 1808, the Perceval family moved to Ealing. They settled on a house called Elm Grove (now demolished) near Ealing Common. This was because Jane, his wife, admired the views of the Surrey hills from it. Perceval himself was a great family man and on the eve of his death was delighted to spend time with them all. On dressing on 10 May 1812, he asked his valet about his day's appointments and on learning there were none, he remarked 'What, not anyone to dinner? Then I am happy, for I shall have a pleasure I very seldom enjoy, of

Spencer Perceval, c.1812. LBE

dining with my family alone.' Even Perceval's enemies gave him credit for having an exemplary private life.

On Monday 11 May 1812, at about 5.15 in the evening, Perceval was entering the lobby of the House of Commons, where a few other men were standing. One of these men, who had been previously in the recess of a doorway in the lobby, drew a small pistol and shot Perceval in the chest. Staggering forward a few steps, the premier fell, but was caught by a number of bystanders. They took him to the room belonging to the Speaker's secretary and William Lynn, a local surgeon, was immediately sent for. Ironically, the two men who went to find Lynn were thought by some to be the killers themselves!

It was already too late. The doctor realized the case was hopeless. All Perceval could say was 'Murder' or 'Murdered'. Twelve minutes after the bullet had entered his left breast, he was dead. Both Lords and MPs came into the death chamber, 'all of them appeared greatly

Elm Grove, Ealing, c.1870. LBE

agitated'. There had been but little effusion of blood externally and the corpse was removed to the Speaker's House.

Meanwhile, what of the assassin? A man who had been passing behind Perceval at the time of the shooting seized the pistol from the assailant, who, making no attempt to escape, then surrendered without any struggle. When asked if he was the murderer, the man replied 'I am that unhappy man', but did so with little emotion. He then went on to mumble something about 'redress of grievances from ministers', which implied he had some bone to pick with the government. His pockets yielded a number of notes, copies of which he had previously distributed to MPs. Another loaded pistol was removed from his person and he was then escorted to an upper chamber and then questioned by a number of magistrates.

Following this he was committed to Newgate for trial. A hackney coach was brought in to the grounds to take him there, but a crowd had gathered outside 'and were so exceedingly troublesome and even dangerous' that an escort of cavalrymen was thought necessary to escort the prisoner to gaol. Some of the crowd even applauded him.

Who was the assassin? Was he a political radical, protesting against what some saw as repressive action against the Luddites in the north of England? Or a Bonapartist sympathizer? Or a member of a conspiracy aimed at revolution? Newspaper speculation on the following days brought forward all sorts of wild theories. The fact that many people were so little disturbed was thought by some to be worrying. Magistrates in the counties were told to be on their guard, and in London, both troops and militia were put on the alert. There was an air of uncertainty and fear. Bloody revolution had occurred in France in 1789 and, without the benefit of hindsight, might occur in England.

They need not have been worried (and on the day after the murder, all such security measures were relaxed). The killer was not part of any wider conspiracy. His name was John Bellingham and he was not a public figure. But his action had made him one overnight. Some saw him as a hero – one man shouted

> *Oh! I will fire my gun tomorrow: I did not think there was an Englishman left that had such a heart. He [Bellingham] could not have shot a greater rascal.*

Facts about Bellingham soon came to light during his trial. He was probably born in St Neots in Huntingdonshire in about 1770. In many ways, he was not an inherently bad man. He was described by those sympathetic towards him thus

> *his general character was that of strict integrity – a kind husband and father – loyal in his political opinions – and punctual in the observance of religious duties; and the whole tenor of his life . . . proves him to have been a well intentioned man.*

Yet Bellingham was weak, obstinate and vindictive. Most of all, he had suffered much and lacked the virtue of stoicism. His lot in life had certainly been as unlucky and as unsuccessful as Perceval's had been the reverse. Bellingham's father had died insane when his son was only 10, and his own ventures had not prospered; as an apprentice, he ran away from his master, as a sailor, his ship sank and as a shop-keeper, he became bankrupt in 1794.

It was then that he went to Archangel and so unwittingly set in motion the events which were to lead him to murder. In Russia he worked as a clerk to a merchant for several years and he began to deal with a Mr Borbecker in the timber trade. Returning to England, Bellingham entered into contracts with Hull merchants who wished to obtain timber from Russia. Unfortunately, Borbecker became bankrupt and the merchants of Hull did not receive their wood. Bellingham was arrested and spent some time in prison.

On his release, he went back to Archangel and began again to make business deals. He also came into conflict with the public authorities, and eventually was thrown into gaol there for debt. He then sought the protection of the British minister there, but without success, because debt was a matter for the Russian authorities alone. When he was released, he returned to England in 1809, full of a deep sense of the wrongs that had been done to him by those in authority.

At first he was peaceable enough, married, had two children and set himself up in business in Liverpool as an insurance broker. He contented himself with writing complaint-filled letters to the British government. No attention was paid to these. Leaving his family, he then went to London in early 1812, ostensibly on a business trip.

Bellingham did not at first intend to kill Perceval. He merely continued to write to ministers, MPs and civil servants, asking them that his grievance be discussed. He received polite, standard letters back from them all. No one would take him seriously. He even informed the Bow Street Runners that if he was not listened to, he would take more direct action. Again, he was ignored and he became even more obsessed with his wrongs and grievances.

In some ways, he seemed fairly normal. Apart from letter writing, he conducted business matters, went to church, visited museums and spent time with acquaintances. He had been staying at lodgings in New Millman Street, near to the Foundling Hospital. His landlady, Mrs Rebecca Robarts, recalled that he had been complaining about money troubles, in which he had been wronged and which threatened to ruin him. Yet in other ways, she found him to be pleasant and well mannered, and he even helped find her child when it went missing. On the day of the crime, they had spent the afternoon looking at paintings, before Bellingham wandered in the direction of Westminster, casually mentioning that he had some business to attend to.

After Bellingham realized that his letter writing was getting him nowhere, he decided that he must take other steps. He reasoned that he had been patient and reasonable and that it was officialdom that was unreasonable. He certainly planned his crime carefully. In early May, he had been seen often in the dining rooms of the Commons, in order to acquaint himself with the place and the people. Access to Parliament was then far more unrestricted than it has become in more recent years and, as long as a visitor looked respectable, security was almost non-existent. He also purchased a pair of pistols and practised firing them in Hampstead. Just before his final action, he received a negative reply from the government on his pleas for compensation. The die was now cast.

When he was put on trial on 15 May, Bellingham freely admitted his guilt. He also said that he knew the consequence of his action. But he was also eager to explain why he had acted in so drastic a fashion.

He said 'I have been denied the redress of my grievances by government; I have been ill treated.' He then told them about how, on business in Russia, he had been wrongfully imprisoned by the Russian authorities there. The trial lasted 8 hours.

Finding Bellingham guilty was therefore easy. There was, in his defence, an attempt to prove that he was insane and therefore unable to plead. Mr Alley, his counsel, brought forward witnesses to try and prove this. One Anne Billett claimed that several witnesses in Liverpool and elsewhere swore to Bellingham's insanity. Yet these came to nothing because no one could be brought forward to prove that, during Bellingham's time in London, he had appeared to be insane. On the contrary, his preparations made for the murder showed him to be as sane as anyone and certainly able to distinguish right from wrong. A tailor came forward to state that Bellingham had asked him to construct side pockets on his suit so he would be able to have easy access to the contents (i.e. his pistols). Witnesses who had been in the lobby at the time of the crime also attested to his guilt.

Since counsel for the accused were only able to examine witnesses and advise the prisoner on points of law, Bellingham had to defend himself. He was more than willing to do so and spoke for 2 hours in his own defence. It must have been a tedious and self-justifying harangue. He said that he had no personal grudge against Perceval, but that he cried out for a settlement of his grievances. He claimed that Lord Gower, the British representative in Russia, would have been his preferred target, as it was Gower who let him down and refused to help a fellow Briton. He then burst out with the following 'Oh, my God, what must his heart be made of! Gentlemen, I appeal to you as men, as fathers, as Christians, if I had not cause of complaint.' The jury took 10 minutes to find he was guilty, a verdict which greatly surprised him, though he was as calm as ever. After the death sentence was passed, there was a lengthy moralistic harangue by the judge about the iniquity of his crime.

In his last few days, Bellingham showed little remorse for his crime. This was because he was content that his wrongs had been avenged, at least in his own mind. However, he did feel sorry for Perceval and his family. The crime of course, was against the government whom he felt should have helped him in Russia, rather than the premier himself. He was also sorry that he would never see his wife and children again in this world, and wrote to them, believing that he and they had much popular sympathy. Bellingham was hanged outside Newgate on 18 May (executions at Tyburn had ceased in 1783). He appeared fully composed and prepared to go through all the final religious ceremonies. He admitted that he had acted alone without any accomplices, but refused to appear contrite. 'His behaviour on the whole was such as apparently to render him, in his last moments, rather an object of interest, than of detestation.' There was no disturbance on the part of the 2,000-strong crowd during the execution. Even so, the government was taking no chances and assembled strong bodies of troops in the locality of Newgate. After all, graffiti such as 'Rescue Bellingham or die!' hinted that a violent rescue attempt might be made.

At 8.00 in the morning, Bellingham was executed. Death was speedy. William Cobbett, a political journalist and enemy of Perceval, noted that there were tears in the eyes of the people in the crowd. He noted that, although the crime was 'a wicked act', it 'had ridded them of one whom they looked upon as the leader amongst those they thought totally bent on the destruction of their liberties'. They could, of course, have been reacting to the courage and calm demeanour in which Bellingham met his end.

After the trial and execution of Bellingham, there was some sympathy for him. No one, of course, denied that he did kill Perceval. Rather, they argued that the swift nature of the judicial process was unfair and that Bellingham was insane and so should not have hanged as he did not know what he was doing. They said that witnesses who could have testified to his character and his mental condition could have been brought had more time been allowed. Other killers whose crimes are related in this book were spared from hanging because of their mental condition. This was because of the change in the law in 1843, following the murder of Sir Robert Peel's secretary by one McNaghten, which recognized that murder by one deemed insane was not the same as a crime perpetrated by a sane man or woman. Yet Bellingham considered himself sane and that his act had been a reasoned response in an attempt to claim redress of his grievances. He was acting reasonably in his opinion, but his actions and subsequent justifications in court would, today, hardly be regarded as a man of sane mind.

Several strange stories circulated shortly after the murder. One was the account of a dream by John Williams, a mining manager in Redruth, Cornwall. Apparently, a week before the event, he dreamt that he was in the lobby of the Commons and saw the crime take place before his very eyes. He had the same dream on the following night. However, he did not recognize the two protagonists in the dream. His son-in-law, when he heard the story, realized that the men in the dream were Perceval and Bellingham, but they did not think anyone would believe such a fantastic tale and so kept it to themselves. Six weeks after the murder, Williams went to visit the

Commons and was able to identify the exact place where Perceval had been shot. The truth of this story is impossible to know, as it was only reported after the crime and to foretell the past is easy. However, Williams did attest in a signed statement that it was true and this was published in *The Times* in 1828.

Lord Gower, who was blamed by Bellingham as the man who refused to assist him in Russia, defended himself in print, in order that the government's probity not be called into question. He argued that he did recall receiving a letter from Bellingham in 1805, asking for help for wrongful imprisonment. However, after making enquiries with both the Russian authorities and the British merchant community, Gower helped to have Bellingham released. This contradicts Bellingham's account of matters and it is impossible to ascertain who was in the right.

As for Perceval, he was buried close to his birthplace in Charlton, Kent, at his wife's request. Politicians of all hues paid their respects. His wife was granted an annual allowance of £2,000. A sum of £50,000 was voted for the family and a monument erected in Westminster Abbey. Jane remarried the son of Ealing's vicar and one of his daughters married Spencer Walpole, who was to become Home Secretary. His four remaining daughters did not marry and lived and died in Ealing; Fredericka, his youngest daughter, was the last to die (in 1900).

All Saints' Church, Ealing, c.1910. Reg Eden's collection

All Saints Church, Ealing Common

But that was not all. Perceval's memory was kept fresh in other ways. On 1 November 1905, 143 years to the day after he had been born, All Saints' Church on Ealing Common was consecrated (funds being provided by Fredericka Perceval) and known as The Spencer Perceval Memorial Church, on land that had been part of the grounds of Elm Grove. Although the idea to call Ealing's main public park Perceval Park was dropped (it was named Walpole Park), more recently, Ealing Council's office block was named Perceval House. There are also a number of other memorials to him, including an English Heritage plaque in Lincoln's Inn and one in St Mary's Church, Ealing. Bellingham is largely forgotten.

Chapter 13

The Hanwell Mystery 1825

This was as mysterious a transaction as had ever come within his knowledge.

In the spring of 1825, the inns of the small village of Hanwell were probably full of talk of one event. That was the 'Mysterious Murder near Hanwell' as *The Times* put it. News must have been lacking for the national newspaper to concern itself with an event in which none of the participants were of any social or political importance.

Robert Chadwell, aged about 60, and variously described as either a sawyer or a wheelwright of Uxbridge, was asked by his master, one of the two basketmakers of Windsor Road, Uxbridge, to deliver a message and payment of a bill, to a man in Ealing. On Friday morning, 25 March 1825, Chadwell did so. He hitched a lift with Mr Tollett, on the Uxbridge coach, along the Uxbridge Road to Ealing; a distance of 7 miles. Chadwell alighted at *The Green Man* inn, Ealing. The message and money were delivered and all that there was left for him to do was to return home.

If he had done so, then no record of Chadwell's errand would have made the national press. However, no doubt pleased he had accomplished it so quickly and easily, Chadwell decided to refresh himself at one or more of the many hostelries which lined the main road. One source says he was accompanied by two other men when he went on his drinking spree. Chadwell became drunk and had to be carried to the stables of *The Green Man* in the afternoon in order to sleep it off. He had been 'seen by many persons in a state of beastly intoxication'.

He soon recovered and entered the taproom, where he remained for some time. He then began to quarrel with one John Brown, wagoner of the Brackley wagon, about him wanting to hitch a ride back on the wagon. Samuel Springall was Brown's fellow wagoner and he came into the inn with William Gladman, the wagoners' lad. They were probably changing their horses and having a break before resuming their journey. Eventually, though, Chadwell and Brown became reconciled, at least temporarily, and Brown offered Chadwell a lift on his wagon. Brown even bought Chadwell a pint of beer, Chadwell not having any money.

They all left the inn at the same time. Then, according to James Herbert, an ostler at the inn, the men fell out and Chadwell was not, after all, allowed to ride in the wagon. Gladman drove the wagon; Brown and Springall walked behind it. They had travelled for about 3 miles on their route, when the Buckinghamshire wagon overtook them. Indeed, it was John Gillett, driver of that wagon, who had made a terrible discovery.

Gillett had found the body of Chadwell at 7.00 that evening, quite dead, by the side of the road, near The Duke of York in Hanwell. The body was still warm, a fact that was corroborated by James Knight, publican. James Price Evans, a Hanwell surgeon, was sent for and examined the body in the same inn, and, amazingly, in light of later discoveries, did not find any obvious cause of death. It must have been a very cursory examination. He declared that death was the result of apoplexy and this result was recorded when the inquest was duly held on 28 March. It was supposed also that a wagon had gone over him. The body was then stripped and, on the same evening, returned to Uxbridge for burial. The crime might have gone un-detected but for the vigilance of a washer-woman who had been told

The Green Man, *Ealing, c.1930.* LBE

to wash Chadwell's clothes. Noticing bloodstains in the underclothes, she contacted the authorities.

The corpse was then examined again, this time by Dr Edward Grimstone of Uxbridge. He came to a different conclusion than that of Evans. After a close survey, he found a wound on the right side of the lower body, apparently caused by a knife, which had penetrated 8 inches into the body. It was this wound which had proved fatal by severing the main artery in two, and would have caused death instantly. Other marks were found on the thighs; these were caused by a blow across by the thighs, made by a whip. A similar injury was found on the left hand, probably received in an attempt to ward off another such blow. These results were confirmed by Mr Samuel Blunt, an Ealing surgeon.

Mr Stirling, the coroner, was told of these facts and so he sent the corpse back to Hanwell and resummoned the same jury. Another inquest was held (on 4 April), when other information was gathered.

According to Gillett, the Brackley wagon had been overtaken at the Hayes Bridge, further along on the road, by the Buckinghamshire wagon. By this time, Springall was driving and the other two were fast asleep in the back of the wagon. Gillett woke Brown and told him that Chadwell was dead, a fact Brown failed to remember.

Mrs Heath, a widow living near *The Duke of York*, claimed she heard a noise in the road just before 7.00. It sounded like men quarrelling; and she also heard the sound of a whip being administered sharply. These sounds soon died away.

John Brown, when summoned to appear at the second inquest, said that they had left Chadwell at *The Green Man* and had been joined by a woman, whom they parted with en route to Hanwell. When they stopped to let her off, Chadwell passed them, allegedly saying 'I am jogging on for Uxbridge'. Suspicion fell most of all on Brown, but *The Times* thought it was groundless.

This time the jury returned a verdict of murder by person or persons unknown.

After the inquest, *The Times* reported:

> *As may be supposed, the above circumstances have not yet ceased to be a topic of conjecture and conversation in the neighbourhood, and many rumours are afloat, which it would be both unwise and unjust to repeat.*

Colonel Clitheroe of Boston House, New Brentford, was the magistrate who investigated the murder. He had Gladman brought to his house for questioning and this revealed 'a number of additional facts'. These were not made known to the public at first. Clitheroe obtained summonses from Sir Richard Birnie (who also assisted Clitheroe in

The Duke of York *(background centre), Hanwell Broadway, c.1870.* LBE

the questioning), in order to have Brown and Springall brought before him for questioning. Their knives were examined but these did not fit the wound. The woman who briefly rode with them was questioned but could add nothing to what was already known. All the witnesses were dismissed. No others who had been on that stretch of road on that evening could be found.

According to *The Times,*

> *Sir R. Birnie said that this was as mysterious a transaction as had ever come within his knowledge. There was no doubt that the deceased had been murdered, but at present, there was nothing to show by whom the act was committed.*

The truth of the matter was never resolved. Did Brown or one of his associates kill Chadwell? They seem to have had, at best, only the slightest of motives. And, given that the quarrel in *The Green Man* was public, the finger of suspicion could not help but be pointed at Brown. No one else was seen in the vicinity of the crime and when Gillett found the body it was warm. If Brown did not kill Chadwell, who did? And why? There was no other suspect with either motive or opportunity, let alone both.

It is possible that Brown may have killed Chadwell in a fit of semi-drunken rage. Brown was probably drunk when he was asleep in the wagon. He is the only man known to have had even the slightest of motives. He may have thrown away the weapon used to kill Chadwell. It seems odd that Chadwell could have overtaken the wagon on foot. After all, he was elderly. Yet this is slight evidence and to try a man for his life on such a basis would be questionable at best. All that can be said is that Brown seems the least unlikely suspect for the murder of Chadwell.

All this would have been of no consolation to Chadwell's widow and the large family he left behind him. It is to be hoped that they were helped by his brother, a manufacturer of beer machines.

Chapter 14

A Policeman's Lot is Not a Happy One
1863

He had been shot in the head at close range and was scarcely recognizable.

ilbert and Sullivan's song from *The Pirates of Penzance* is meant as comedy, but it also contains an element of tragedy. Many policemen and women have been so 'unhappy' as to have been killed in the line of duty. PC William Davey was one of this unfortunate band and it is his (and his wife's) 'unhappy lot' which we shall now investigate. Acton in 1863 was still a large village outside London, although it was on the verge of expansion and this entailed building work. It was this which led to Davey's fate.

The 40-year-old policeman was on his beat on Bollo Lane on the afternoon of Monday 19 January. There had been little of note to report until he encountered two men carrying planks of wood. He asked them to account for the wood. When they were unable to do so, he proceeded to try and arrest them. One of them, Joseph Brooks, a 25-year-old labourer and a powerfully built man, threw the wood at him and escaped. The other, his brother, Isaac Brooks, aged 23, who was also a labourer, was held, but was released after a few minutes. Davey reported the incident to his immediate superior, Sergeant Arthur Bonnick, at about 6 o'clock. They decided that they would have to investigate further and visit the building site belonging to Mr Saunderson at Bollo Bridge Road, from which the wood had been taken. However, as it was dinner time, Bonnick gave Davey permission to return home and have dinner there. It would be the last time he would see his colleague alive.

Davey and Martha, his wife, lived at Petherton Villas, Avenue Road. This was a semi-detached house. Davey arrived home shortly after 8.30. Scarcely had he begun his meal in the back parlour when the door bell rang and his wife answered it. The caller, presumably

Bollo Lane, Acton, 2005. The author

standing some way away as he could not be identified, asked to see her husband, so she disappeared into the house while Davey went out to see who wanted him. It was his last action.

Martha Davey then heard a loud blast, as if from a gun being discharged nearby. Leaving the house she found the corpse of her husband on the threshold of their home. He had been shot in the head at close range and was scarcely recognizable: at least he had died almost instantly. She gave the alarm and people gathered around.

The investigation proceeded swiftly. Bonnick arrived on the scene at about 8.40 and told his superiors what he had seen as soon as possible. In the early hours of the following morning, Inspectors Searl and Scotney, went to No. 1 Chapel Place, Back Common, Turnham Green, the home of the Brooks brothers. Both were at home. Isaac let them in and they found Joseph in bed. Both trembled. When asked if they had any firearms, Joseph said 'I have none; I had a gun, but I left it at the shop at Acton.' Unfortunately for him, when the police searched the room, they found a one-barrelled gun in his bed and he stated that he had forgotten it was there. Worse still, when he was dressing, a powder horn fell from his cord jacket. However, he laughed and joked with the police.

Joseph Brooks explained that, though the gun was dirty, it had been used last week, but not since. He also explained that it had been pledged at a pawnbroker's in Hammersmith, being only redeemed on the previous evening. Isaac's wife said that she and Jane Lake, Joseph's fiancée, had been to the shop to reclaim the gun. William Ayres, the pawnbroker, said it was pawned on 17 January and redeemed at about 7.30 on the evening of the murder by Miss Lake and Mrs Brooks. He remembered the gun was clean when it left his shop. All this seemed evidence enough for the police to have the Brooks brothers remanded for the murder of PC Davey.

The two were indicted at the Old Bailey on 2 March. Various witnesses claimed to have seen two men lurking outside Petherton Villas just before the murder. One said that a man was hiding in a ditch and that his companion was Joseph Brooks. Martha Davey thought the voice of the man who called for her husband was that of Isaac Brooks. Just after the murder, a man was seen running away in the direction of Turnham Green. Isaac was seen amongst the circle of men who surrounded the corpse just after the crime. Jane Lake was accused of being an accessory for burning a hat belonging to Joseph that might have been crucial evidence. In their defence, the Brooks brothers swore that they had been at work on the day of the murder, but had returned home at about 6.00 and had not left the house since. Yet it was thought that the evidence was strong enough for them to be further remanded for trial in the following month.

Mr Baron Wilde presided at the trial on 8 April. The Brooks brothers pleaded not guilty. They appeared cool and calm throughout, not exchanging a word throughout the trial. In the interim, Jane Lake had been freed as there was no evidence that she had been an accessory to murder.

The prosecution brought forward a number of witnesses to give evidence against the Brooks brothers. Georgiana Winning told how she had seen them running home at about 6.00, presumably after

Avenue Road, Acton, 1967. LBE

their first encounter that evening with Davey. Another witness said he saw a man running from the scene of the murder towards Turnham Green. Another man said he saw a man, possibly Joseph, with a gun on the most direct path from Turnham Green to Petherton Villas, at about 8.00. Others thought they saw him walking or lurking in the vicinity of Petherton Villas, but were not completely certain, as it had been dark. Several recalled seeing Isaac with a group of people with the corpse after the murder.

Then Jane Lake, in a very emotional state, gave her evidence. She said that Joseph told her to go to the pawnbroker's shop that evening to redeem his gun as he wanted to sell it. She did, and on her return, gave it to him. He then left the house and told her not to follow. He said he was going to sell it in Hammersmith. The time was perhaps 7.40, but Jane was uncertain. She thought he returned at about 8.00, very hot and sweaty, after presumably having run most of the way. Then there was the evidence of the gun. The pawnbroker said that the gun had been fired sometime after he had returned it to Jane, as it had been clean on its return, yet was dirty when the police examined it. Finally, a surgeon deposed that the type of ammunition which had been used to kill Davey was of the type which would have fitted Joseph's gun. Thus the prosecution rested their case.

The defending counsel said that there was no motive why Joseph or Isaac should have killed Davey. One had been sought, but none had been found. It was then argued that, even if there had been one, it would have been physically impossible for them to have killed Davey. Since, following his repossession of the gun, Joseph had only been absent for 20 minutes, according to Jane Lake, he could not have had the time to commit the crime. It was almost a mile from his home to Petherton Villas and to have run nearly 2 miles and killed Davey would have been impossible. Furthermore, the witnesses for the prosecution had talked of seeing a man, or men, lurking, which hardly tallied with someone running at top speed. Discrepancies in the witnesses' stories were also pointed out. Finally, it was said that the prosecution's case was based on circumstantial evidence and that it was for the prosecution to prove beyond all doubt that Joseph or Isaac were guilty.

Baron Wilde summed up that it was Joseph who was facing the capital charge. He reminded the jury that circumstantial evidence could be thought as sound proof of guilt, but added that it was not clear that the Brooks had stolen the wood, as it was only Davey who had thought so. Yet, there was no evidence that Joseph had tried to sell the gun to anyone when he said he was going out to do so and the shot in Davey was of the same type as that in his gun.

The jury, after 20 minutes, found Joseph to be guilty and acquitted Isaac of any wrongdoing. Joseph said nothing to this verdict. Wilde, donning black silk, stated that the murder was coolly planned and executed, rather than being done on the spur of the moment under provocation. With that, Joseph was sent down and his sister, who was in the gallery, shrieked.

Yet unanswered questions remained. What Joseph's motive had been remains unknown. The theft of wood was a relatively minor offence, and even if the Brooks had been guilty of such a theft, Joseph's murderous response would seem to have been totally disproportionate. Furthermore, how could Joseph move so quickly to kill Davey and then return home? Perhaps the answer is that Jane Lake may have underestimated the time he was gone, as presumably she lacked a watch or clock. On the other hand, why did Joseph leave home on the evening in question? No one testified to him having tried to sell them the gun as he claimed. And where did he fire it, as it undoubtedly had been discharged? Both cases for prosecution and defence seem inadequate. Yet, despite these question marks, Brooks confessed to the murder a few days after he had been found guilty. A solicitor for the prosecution wrote to *The Times* and noted that Brooks had stolen the wood and was a deserter, presumably from the Army, and so his offences were not minimal.

The result, though, was that Joseph Brooks was hanged by the neck until he was dead, one of the last public executions.

Chapter 15

Murder Most Foul
1880

It is impossible to conceive a more atrocious or a more cruel crime.

Of course, all murder is foul, but the killing of a child is especially so, and, though there are other accounts of murders of children in this book, this one was particularly brutal, since there was a sexual dimension to it. What made this case even more shocking than it would have been already is the fact that it came out of the blue. No murder had been committed in Acton for seventeen years – the last being that already related, the murder of PC Davey. Would that Acton had been so free from murder in more recent years!

The day began ordinarily enough for the families involved. It was Friday 22 October 1880. John Shepherd, painter and decorator of Herbert Villa, Cowper Road, Acton, had reason to be thankful. He had sold a house the day before for £150 and was going to Norwood in south London with his second wife to bank the cash. Before departing, they left their four children at home. Ada, the eldest, aged just over 10, and a child of his first marriage, was to remain at home

Acton Central Station, 2005. The author

Cowper Road, Acton, 2005. The author

while the three younger ones were to attend school (schooling was then only compulsory to the age of 10).

There was another person in the house that day. He was George Pavey, a painter aged 29, who lived in Manchester Street, Notting Hill, with his wife and nine-month-old baby. Whereas Shepherd had been materially successful, Pavey was down on his luck. He also suffered from infirmity in one arm and one leg. In the previous six months Shepherd had been giving Pavey jobs to do, so that the Paveys would not be destitute, as trade was slack. That day, Pavey was asked to paint some ladders and to remain at the house until Shepherd returned. Although Pavey had never been left in the house in such circumstances, he was trusted by his employer, who considered him to be 'a well conducted, orderly man', in whom he 'had every confidence'. Just the day before, Shepherd had told him about his success in selling a house. Meanwhile, in the afternoon, Mrs Pavey was preparing the tea for her husband.

Pavey left home for work at 8.30. After detailing his duties, Mr and Mrs Shepherd set off at about 11.30 to catch a train at Acton Central for Norwood, and, their business concluded, returned home at about 6.35 in the evening. When they arrived, after walking from the station, they were in for a terrible shock. The house was in darkness and the back door was fastened. Receiving no reply after knocking, Shepherd used his latch-key to gain entry. As he entered the kitchen after walking through the passage and looked for a light, he stumbled over something on the floor.

It was the body of his daughter, Ada. She was lying on the hearth-rug in front of the fireplace, but was cold and rigid. Finding a neighbour, they put on a light and the awful reality sank in. His daughter was lying on her back in a pool of blood, quite dead. A handkerchief had been placed over her face and her throat had been cut and there were bruises around the face, including a black eye. A blood-stained kitchen knife was found nearby.

The police and a doctor were quickly summoned. Dr Clement Murrell of Churchfield Road examined the corpse. According to one report, 'On examination a terrible gash was found in the throat, near to the jugular vein and carotid artery, which must have caused the poor child to have bled to death speedily.' He also estimated that death had taken place at about 3 o'clock. The girl had also been sexually assaulted or, to use a Victorian term, 'brutally outraged'. The police examined the house and found that a room on the first floor had been broken into. Shepherd's money-box had been opened and searched, though fruitlessly, as he had removed the contents to take up to London that very day.

Of Pavey, there was, however, no sign. He had been last seen at 3.30, walking down Birkbeck Road and into the Uxbridge Road. Enquiries revealed that he had not been home that afternoon, though his wife was expecting him. Inspector Savage waited there until one in the morning, but Pavey did not return. The police began to scour the district for him. As he was the principal suspect, there was concern that a lynch mob might deal out rough justice to him, such was 'the utmost indignation' which was 'felt against the perpetrator of such a foul crime upon a defenceless child'.

After two days, Pavey was apprehended. He had spent those days wandering about London, staying in lodging houses and reaching the Hendon Workhouse on Sunday 24 October, and it was here where the police found him and took him to Edgware Police Station and finally to Paddington Police Station for questioning. He had read an account of the murder but did not think he matched the description of the wanted man. On the following day, he made his appearance at Hammersmith Police Court, where extra police were needed to hold back the crowds, such was the horror and contempt which was felt towards him. Pavey bore such glances with fortitude. The first witness to be examined before the magistrate was Shepherd, who told how he had discovered the body. He added that the three other children had come home for lunch at about noon, but then returned to school

Churchfield Road, Acton, c.1900. LBE

afterwards. In the afternoon, once school was over, they had tried to return home, but could not, so had stayed with a neighbour in Milton Road.

Dr Murrell was the next witness and he discussed the nature of the injuries and the cause of death. He suggested that the table knife was the weapon used. The police stated that the handkerchief over the dead girl's face was Pavey's, a fact he had admitted himself. Although he denied knowing about the bloody knife, bloodstains were found on his clothing.

Later that morning, the inquest was held in the Station Hotel in Churchfield Road. Those who had spoken at the police court made similar statements again, but there was also some fresh evidence. George Eckford, confectioner and tobacconist of Churchfield Road, stated that Ada had bought some sweets from his shop at 2.00 on the afternoon of the murder. About 45 minutes later, John Trindell, a builder, went to Herbert Villas to try and borrow a ladder, but no one answered the door. A lad, William Shepherd (no known relation), said he saw Pavey walk down Birkbeck Road at 3.20.

The coroner then asked the jury to make up their minds. He reminded them that the evidence against Pavey was circumstantial, but that it was difficult to see how anyone else could have killed Ada. The jury found that wilful murder had been committed by Pavey and they wished to express their deepest sympathy with the Shepherd family. Meanwhile, Pavey issued a statement in his defence. He claimed that after Ada had left the house to buy sweets, a short, bearded man in working dress had come to the house and told him that Shepherd wanted to see him at the Uxbridge Road Railway Station, Shepherd's Bush (now defunct). He went there as requested, but found it was a hoax. On returning, he found Ada's body. He had been gone for about 45 minutes. The reason why he did not at once contact the police was that he had 'been previously convicted of assaults upon children, he felt that the case would look black against him'. Unsurprisingly, Shepherd had been unaware of his record before now.

Pavey was examined before magistrates on 1 November at Hammersmith Police Court. Again, the hearing was well attended by the public. Mr Poland called the remainder of the witnesses in order to present a complete case against the accused, whilst Mr Farman cross-examined witnesses in order to try and defend Pavey. One piece of new evidence was that Shepherd missed a pair of boots he had left at home. These were later presented to a Notting Hill pawnbroker by Pavey. No one had seen the mysterious man whom Pavey alleged decoyed him away. The milkman stated that he had called at Herbert Villas at about 2.50 and no answer was received. The defence focused on Pavey's story about being decoyed from the house and Farman stated that the evidence was too weak for Pavey to be sent to the Old Bailey for trial. However, the magistrate decided to commit him for trial.

Pavey was optimistic about his chances. He was allowed to see his wife and told her:

> *You go to Madame Tussaud's at once with my clothes, trousers, waist coat – everything, and sell them; you will get at least two sovereigns for them. Directly I get out of this – and I'm sure I shall – I shall go to every place I can think of, and exhibit myself for so much. Look here, missis, I shall make my fortune.*

Meanwhile the funeral of Ada Shepherd was well attended by many sympathizers, though rain fell as the burial took place.

The trial took place on 24 November. Pavey pleaded not guilty. It was put forward that the motive for the murder was the money that Shepherd was thought to have had in the box upstairs, and which it was thought Pavey knew about. It was suggested that Ada was violated and killed before the attempt at theft occurred. Pavey's blood-stained clothes were referred to, as was his flight from justice. The defence rested on Pavey's story about how he had been called away, suggested that the bloodstains were caused by a nose bleed and asked that Pavey's previous assaults on children be overlooked. The jury was unconvinced and took only a few minutes to find him guilty. Mr Justice Hawkins donned his black cap and addressed Pavey:

> *It is impossible to conceive a more atrocious or a more cruel crime than that which you have been convicted ... God knows what could have possessed you to commit that atrocious cruelty in violating the person of that poor helpless child and afterwards to murder her.*

Shortly before Pavey was hanged, on 13 December, alleged accounts of his dying speech and confession were being hawked around Acton. Pavey had previously fully admitted his guilt and had written to Shepherd to ask his forgiveness. He was in regular attendance at the prison chapel and paid great attention to the ordinary (or chaplain) there. An article in one magazine tried to argue that Pavey was not at fault because he had a diseased brain and so had no moral restraint. Such reasoning was viewed as disgusting by *The Acton Gazette*.

Chapter 16

Who Murdered Sarah Higgs?
1895

She was lying here in the canal within sight of our windows, only 50 yards away and we knew nothing about it.

For the middle classes, the nineteenth century was a golden age for servants. Most professional people, businessmen and shopkeepers, as well as those of independent means, possessed at least one; most had two or three domestic servants. These were usually female, so could not command the wages of their male equivalents. Kensington apart, in the late Victorian era, Ealing had the highest number of servants per head of population. The lot of servants was variable, but few had the fate of Sarah Higgs.

In the local press, in late February 1895, came the following paragraph:

> *At the beginning of last week much painful excitement was caused in Yiewsley and the surrounding locality, by the discovery, in the Grand Junction Canal, near Horton Bridge, of the dead body of Sarah Jane Higgs ...*

Sarah Higgs had been born in about 1870 at Yiewsley, Middlesex, and her parents still lived there in 1895, at Thatcher's Cottages, near Horton Bridge. Since the summer of 1894, she had been employed as a housemaid at Mrs Josephine Draper's house at Mount Park Road, Ealing, and received an annual salary of £16, paid monthly. She appeared to be 'a quiet, well behaved, respectable young woman' and her mother said she was cheerful and industrious. As a child she had attended the local National School, leaving at 13. She had then worked as a servant in various posts – at the West Drayton station-master's, then at Uxbridge, then in London, before working at Ealing.

That her character was golden was not strictly true. It later appeared that she had given birth sometime in the past, and the father acknowledged the baby as his, contributing towards its maintenance until the baby's death. Although the father was unknown, it was said to be a man who lived near her mother's house. Furthermore, she was three months pregnant at the time of death – or, as the newspapers delicately put it 'her mistress had reason to suspect her condition'. In fact, Mrs Draper had intended to speak to her on this matter.

She never had the chance. On the evening of Thursday 2 January 1895, Sarah left the house. At first this went unnoticed. Thursday was her usual evening off and she had talked to Matilda Baker, a fellow servant, of catching the 8.17 pm train to visit her parents at Yiewsley and to return by 10 o'clock, which was when she was required to be at her employer's. There would have been time for her to have made a short visit and then to return. West Drayton Station was and is only about 10 minutes walk at most, from where her parents lived. She had been wearing a round sailor hat, a dark dress and jacket and a white silk handkerchief. She also stated that the reason for the visit was to visit a dressmaker there.

What happened on the evening of 2 January is impossible to say with complete certainty. What is clear is that she did not travel by the 8.17 train, as she was seen in Ealing Broadway just before 9 o'clock. It would then have been impossible for her to have gone to Yiewsley and returned for 10 o'clock. Such behaviour was unusual and Sarah had never failed to return before, except when she had to take a few days off in the previous August, due to illness. On the following day, Sarah's sister came to Mrs Draper's house and took away Sarah's belongings, though no money was found, despite Sarah being said to be reasonably affluent. Mrs Draper found some medicine bottles in her employee's room and an unfinished letter to her half-sister,

Mount Park Road, Ealing, 1962. LBE

concerning some trinkets she planned to give to her. None of those who knew her at Yiewsley had seen her there. Meanwhile, the police made enquiries at lodging houses, without any positive result.

It was on 25 February that Thomas Clayton, butcher and fruiterer of Yiewsley High Street, made the shocking discovery. He had been walking along the canal tow path, near Horton Bridge and less than 100 yards from where Sarah's mother lived, and saw what he at first thought to be bundle of rags floating in a gap in the ice-covered water. He thought nothing of it and passed by. However, on passing the same way again, later in the day, he examined the object and found that it was a corpse. PC Cruikshank was summoned and took charge. Among the crowd who gathered there, a man shouted 'There has been foul play here.' The corpse's outer skirt had been removed but otherwise it was fully clothed. Sarah's mother said of the tragedy:

Only think that while we have been wondering where she was or where she could have got to, that she was lying here in the canal within sight of our windows, only 50 yards away and we knew nothing about it.

The inquest was held later that day at the *De Burgh Hotel*, very near to West Drayton Railway Station. After identifying the body and having heard from Martha Higgs, Sarah's mother, that the family had not seen her since August 1894, when Sarah had been ill, the main point under discussion was the cause of death. Dr William Hayden said that the face and the lower part of the body were covered in mud from the bottom of the canal, but he thought that the corpse had not been held down in it. It was only slightly decomposed. He had also found, on closer examination, that there was a frontal head wound about 1½ inches long, which had broken one bone and fractured another. There was also a wound at the back of the head, which had not broken any bones. These blows had been inflicted when Sarah was alive, by a fall or a blow. She had not drowned, as there was no water in the lungs, but had been in the water for at least six weeks. The stomach was healthy, but there was no food in it. She was three months pregnant. The inquest was then adjourned in order to ascertain Sarah's last movements and to gather other pertinent information.

The adjourned inquest, took place at the same location, but with the police present, a week later. Inspector Nash, a detective inspector, and his colleagues had been making investigations. The adjourned inquest lasted 3 hours. A number of witnesses were questioned.

Mary Farr, a servant at 18 Eccleston Road, Ealing Dean, reported that she was a friend of Sarah's and that they often spent their leisure time together. On 16 December, on their way back from Acton, they met a man, whom Sarah referred to as her 'young man', but she did

Lyric Theatre, Ealing Broadway, c.1900. Reg Eden's collection

not know his name. On the night of her disappearance, they had met in Ealing Broadway at 8.20 and walked to Ealing Common railway station, then back again, meeting another female friend outside the Lyric Theatre on Ealing Broadway. Mary then left them at about 9.15. She could not identify the man seen on 16 December, as she had only seen the back of his head. He was about 30, had been wearing a light coat, black felt hat and black trousers; he possibly worked in a shop. She added that Sarah seemed cheerful and did not think anything out of the usual was in the offing.

William Hammond, labourer of St Mary's Cottages, Yiewsley, stated that he had seen Sarah loitering near Horton Bridge early one morning, apparently looking for a lost possession – perhaps her outer skirt. He had known her for five years, but claimed he had never spoken to her, as 'I have got enough to do with the one at home'. When he returned to the same spot, 20 minutes later, she had vanished. Unfortunately he did not remember on what day it was, only 'after Christmas'.

Charles Butler of No. 3 Eastwood's Cottages, Yiewsley, who was possibly a labourer, had walked out with Sarah on three occasions in the summer of 1894. The last was on the August Bank Holiday. He had been with her and Ada, his sister, at the Lyric Theatre, but, though 'we were friendly towards each other', he stressed that 'he was never guilty of any improper conduct' with her and that he 'did not know much' about her. He had not seen her since and did not know if she was seeing another man.

It certainly seems that Sarah was seeing another man. Ellen Downes, a servant working at Eaton Rise, and an old friend of Sarah's, said that Sarah intended to visit the Metropolitan Music Hall in London on Boxing Day 1894 and she was not going alone. She had expected to see Sarah on 30 December, but had not. Sarah's sister said that she knew who she was walking out with and referred to him as 'the biggest scamp out'. She did not identify him. This other man had been friends with Sarah since at least November, and this man was not Charlie. Charlie was clearly Charles Butler, as a servant recalled that Sarah said she had not seen him since August, which agreed with Charles's own account. There was uncertainty whether the man in question was from Ealing or not. Ellen certainly thought so, but others disagreed.

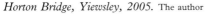

One possible clue – or red herring – came from Algernon Good-enough, booking clerk at West Drayton Station. He said that at 11.00

Horton Bridge, Yiewsley, 2005. The author

at night on 19 January he had heard a woman's screams from the direction of Horton Bridge. He thought it might be a domestic assault, though another witness said they were merely noises made by rowdy youths leaving a nearby pub. When Goodenough saw two constables, they said that the route was not on their beat, so could not investigate. Yet it was believed that Sarah had been starved for two weeks before entering the water, which would tally with Goodenough's statement.

Dr Hayden, who had had time to make another examination, was able to give further evidence. Another fracture at the front of the head wound was found. He said that the cause of death was shock to the nervous system caused by concussion to the brain and spinal cord, being caused by the blow to the back of the head. The body had been in the water for some time and so it was impossible to tell if all the blows had been made at the same time. There was some debate as to whether the death was suicide, caused by Sarah leaping from the bridge and hitting her head on the side of the bridge. Hayden said that Sarah was unconscious, but not dead when she entered the water. The jury only needed a short consultation before reaching the verdict of 'Wilful murder against some person or persons unknown'. Her mother was 'sure Sarah had been murdered and that she had been lured down there for that purpose'.

The killer was never found. The motive for the murder, though, is clear enough. Sarah was pregnant and she had told the prospective father about it. He was not in a position to marry her, or did not wish to do so. Perhaps he was already married or was in a situation in which the scandal of the result of his illicit affair would have been harmful. He may have met her at the Lyric on 2 January, and suggested she go to West Drayton with him. Perhaps he suggested elopement or marriage? This would tie in with the absence of money in her room, as he may have suggested she take it with her. Having lured her there, he must have held her prisoner somewhere (but where? – perhaps a shed or outhouse – certainly nowhere that anyone might conceivably visit) for about two weeks, before deciding on what to do. It is possible that 19 January was the date of the murder and, having wounded her, he threw her from the bridge, where she sank. The delay in the body being discovered was caused by the frosty weather, with ice covering the canal until late February.

Who killed her? Probably not Charles Butler, who had not seen her for months, though he did live near to the scene of the crime. William Hammond? Possibly, possibly not. He had motive (being married already) and was near the scene of the crime. He was vague about when he saw her, though this is not necessarily a sign of guilt, but merely bad memory. He may have been her lover, but the question

The De Burgh Arms, *Yiewsley, 2005.* The author

remains about where he hid her and how she could have been hidden for so long. As both men were labourers, they could hardly appear as the shopkeeper's assistant who had been identified as Sarah's beau. Unless, of course, they had changed into their Sunday best, as one would when courting. It is a pity that Sarah's sister did not name her current lover. Whether this line of enquiry was pursued, we do not know. No more was revealed to the public of any police investigation which surely must have followed the announcement at the inquest, nor do surviving police files help much. It seems we will probably never know the truth.

90

Chapter 17

Murder at the Theatre 1897

He seemed to me to be rather mad, and had a wild, peculiar look about his eyes.

Most murders do not involve the great and good. One exception was Perceval. Another was a man who, though he resided near Ealing, was slain in London and whose tale is about to unfold. In 1897, the year of Queen Victoria's Diamond Jubilee, William Terriss, whose real name was William Lewin, seemed to have it all. He was rich – his estate was worth £18,809 and he lived at Bedford Road, in the fashionable suburb of Bedford Park, in the parish of Acton. Terriss was a successful actor, starring in plays at the Adelphi Theatre, principally in nautical roles, at which he was outstanding, but also in Shakespeare, in which he was creditable. Married for nearly three decades, he had three children, one of whom was beginning to make a successful stage career for herself; he also had a mistress, an actress called Jessie Millward. Finally, he played a significant role in his local community. Could life be any better for the 50 year old? Perhaps not, but it was nearing its climax.

In December 1897, Terriss was playing the part of Lewis Dumont, a Federal spy during the American Civil War, in *Secret Service* by William Gillette (who also wrote a play titled *Sherlock Holmes* and invented the catchphrase 'Elementary, my dear Watson'). His character was working in the Confederate capital of Richmond, where he was also involved with a Southern Belle, played by Jessie Millward. In her private life, she had been troubled by nightmares in which Terriss was calling out to her from a locked room, and as she released him, he fell.

On the evening of 16 December, Terriss and John Graves, a surveyor, left Jessie's flat to go to the theatre, just before 7.00. They left the cab at the Adelphi's stage door on Maiden Lane and Terriss took out a key to unlock the door. When he had done this, he was approached by a stranger. The man moved like lightning and stabbed

Bedford Road, Bedford Park, Acton, 1968. LBE

Terriss four times. One wound was just below his heart. According to accounts, Terriss cried 'My God! He has stabbed me!' or 'Oh my God! I am stabbed!' followed by 'Sis! Sis!' Terriss then sank to his knees. Jessie Millward arrived just in time to hear the words she had also heard in her dreams. Although Terriss was carried inside the theatre and doctors called for, he was dead within 20 minutes. A crowd soon gathered and the commissionaire apprehended the murderer, who made no effort to flee. Graves said 'I charge this man with stabbing Mr Terriss.'

That man was Richard Archer Prince, a 32-year-old unmarried and unemployed minor actor, of Eaton Court, Buckingham Palace Road. He had been born in Scotland and had had a number of minor acting jobs in both Scotland, London (at the Adelphi) and on tour. He had had to take labouring work when money was short.

As he was taken away, he told Graves, in Constable Bragg's company, why he committed the crime: 'In revenge. Mr Terriss prevented me from getting employment. He has blackmailed me for ten years.' There was, of course, no evidence for either of these assertions.

He was charged at the Bow Street Police Court on the following day with the murder. Graves gave evidence of the attack on his friend. The case was remanded and there was great hostility shown towards

Prince. At the inquest on 20 December, the jury gave a verdict of wilful murder by Prince and he was committed for trial.

Prince's sanity was doubtful. Although he claimed that he killed Terriss because the latter stopped him from gaining any money from the Actors' Benevolent Fund, this was mere fantasy. In reality, Terriss had been helpful towards Prince, as was proved by the Fund's secretary, one Mr Colston. Terriss had written that he knew Prince and thought him a hard-working actor. Prince had been awarded sums of money from the Fund since 1892. Before his death, Terriss had confided in a friend that he thought Prince was harassing him. He certainly had written to him, as an envelope was found with Prince's address on, and in Terriss's handwriting, but the contents were unknown.

Those who knew Prince certainly thought him a little mad. Colston said:

> the prisoner greatly resembled the conventional stage villain in dress and appearance. He seemed to me to be rather mad, and had a wild, peculiar look about his eyes on occasions when I have been talking to him in my office.

Others who knew him thought he was moody and had a peculiar look in his eyes and might be a little 'wrong in the head'. Prince's poverty might not have helped. He was in arrears with his rent and ate but little. Otherwise, he was quiet and respectable.

The crime seems to have been planned for some time. Harry Nicholls, a colleague and neighbour of Terriss, gave evidence that Prince had been seen lurking near the theatre for some days, in order to meet Terriss. The night before the murder, Prince rushed up to Nicholls on the latter's departure from the theatre, thinking he was Terriss, and, on finding he was not, asked him where Terriss was. Nicholls said he did not know and told him to clear off. Prince had also been seen in and around Bedford Park, attempting to discover where Terriss lived. He asked one resident, Mr Holloway, where Terriss lived, but he would not say. In any case, Terriss had been staying in his London flat at that time. There was speculation as to whether Prince planned to commit the murder in Bedford Park. It would certainly have been possible to have killed him there and to have easily escaped; assuming Prince wanted to escape after his one moment of fame.

Terriss's funeral was held the day after the inquest. It was a grand affair. Crowds thronged the streets in which the funeral procession of fourteen mourning coaches and over a hundred private carriages passed, starting at Bedford Road. Curtains were drawn as a mark of

Plaque to William Terriss, the Adelphi, 2005.
The author

respect. Those sending wreaths included Lord Rosebery, a former prime minister, and the wealthy Rothschilds. Jessie Millward also attended, one of the few women to do so, as it was then unusual for women to attend funerals. Terriss was buried at Brompton Cemetery. A memorial service was held in the Chapel Royal in the Savoy.

Terriss's loss was hard felt in the locality in which he had lived for sixteen years. The late actor had given generously both to friends who were hard up and to the poor each winter. He had also lobbied the council to have electric street lighting in Bedford Park. Floods of letters and verbal expressions of sympathy were received by Terriss's family. Sir Henry Irving remarked 'I feel sure the whole theatrical profession join with me in mourning over the tragic and untimely end of our dear friend, who was a universal favourite'.

The trial of Prince took place on 13 January 1898. Prince pleaded guilty but added that he had been under great provocation. There was some initial debate as to whether Prince would defend himself, or whether he would use the counsel that was offered him. He eventually chose the latter, and Messrs Sands and Kyd appeared on his behalf. He also had to change his plea, which was one unknown in law, and finally pleaded not guilty.

The case for the prosecution was simple. Prince had conceived a hatred of Terriss, thinking he was blackmailing him, depriving him of financial aid and employment, although he was completely deluded in these beliefs. As to the events leading up to the crime itself, Prince came down to London in October, after being sacked from a theatrical group, where he told the manager that he was his other enemy, and on being asked who the first was Prince replied 'One at the Adelphi. Terriss, the dirty dog.'

Once in the capital, he bought a knife and sought out Terriss, asking that a letter to him be delivered at the stage door. This was done. Terriss recommended Prince to the Benevolent Fund and Prince received small sums of money. Yet on 16 December, he was told that the Fund would grant him no more money. He then returned to his lodgings at Eaton Court, where he was living in poverty, in a state of despair and left again at 4.00 in order to await Terriss at the theatre. The murder was then committed, as previously described. Witnesses were produced to testify to what occurred.

The facts were not disputed by the defence. Their aim was to show that Prince was not responsible for his actions. Members of his family testified that he had been vain, angry and bad tempered as a child. One of Prince's relations had died in a lunatic asylum. More reputable evidence came from other theatrical managers who had employed Prince. As with Terriss, they claimed that Prince had accused them of blackmailing him. Then there was the medical evidence supplied by a number of doctors who had examined him. Dr Bastian attested that Prince was of unsound mind and therefore, for the safety of the public, should be placed in an asylum. He was said to be suffering from delusions of persecution and that, although he knew what he was doing when he killed Terriss, he was unable to know the difference between right and wrong. He was probably suffering from a form of paranoid schizophrenia, with his conviction that he had enemies conspiring against him and his violent behaviour based on these beliefs.

The jury agreed with the doctors; and that though Prince was undoubtedly guilty of murder, he was not, because of his mental condition, responsible for it. It was therefore ordered he be conveyed to an asylum. When the verdict was read out in court, Prince, who was certainly able to follow the proceedings, asked the judge that he be allowed to convey his thanks to all concerned. He was not allowed to do so. Prince was eventually sent to Broadmoor Criminal Lunatic Asylum, where he became the conductor of the inmates' orchestra. He died there in 1937.

Chapter 18

'Yet Every Man Kills the Thing he Loves' 1909

I had suspicions that he was not running straight.

Oscar Wilde's well-known line certainly seems to have been appropriate here, in one of the several cases in this book where a man kills his lover or wife. Although Edwardian guides to Acton liked to portray the place as 'rus in urbe' (countryside in the city), it was far from being a tranquil rural dwelling place. However, it was true that crime was usually of a petty nature – horses were mistreated, cats poisoned, lads threw stones at the library's windows, there were drunk and disorderlies and even some prostitution. Acton was socially divided, with pockets of working class housing in the Steyne and in south Acton. It is to the latter that we shall turn. Since the 1870s, this part of Acton was known as Soapsud Island on account of the huge number of small laundries which were located there. It had been known as Klondyke on account of its 'rough and ready character', but there was also 'respectability, at least in some parts'. Saturday nights were 'probably the time to find the streets at their worst, and to witness anything interesting or exciting of a domestic character'. Yet, even so, what happened on 7 August 1909 was exceptional.

In this district was situated Orchard Cottage, Colville Road, inhabited by the White family, who seemed ordinary enough. Edmund White, a former soldier, who now worked at the Army and Navy Stores as a carpenter, was the head of the household. He was married and had three sons and three daughters. Of the daughters, it is May, 'a round-featured and pleasant looking girl of twenty' to whom we now turn. She worked as a photographic assistant, first in Wyndham's on Bollo Lane, and, since early 1909, at Wakefield's in Brentford. Her employer, Mr Wakefield, described her as 'one of the most kindly and lovable girls. She was of a most careful and thoughtful disposition and was so gentle she would never hurt a flower.'

Acton Green, c.1910. LBE

The most important facet of her life was, however, her association
with Jack Bee. He was a young grocer's assistant, apparently aged 28,
who was employed at Acton Supply Stores. Their friendship dated
from about 1907. May knew little about Bee's background, nor had
she met any of his relatives. Her father later recalled, 'There was a bit
of a mystery about him: he had no relations living, and we knew little
of his history.' But, given his excellent character – 'very good natured
and free with his money' – this did not seem to matter. He had
showered her with gifts, such as a useful bicycle. When she introduced
him to her parents, there were smiles all round and her father
approved of their being engaged. Bee was a regular visitor at the
White home. He later improved his prospects by becoming a manager
of a store in Pimlico.

All was going well for the young couple until Easter 1909. Bee
asked May's father if he could take her to the seaside for the long
holiday weekend. Her father granted him permission – such was the
liberal nature of the Edwardian period. But, quite unexpectedly, Bee
did not meet May as planned. Instead, he sent a lad with a message to
her, to ask for her to meet him. May's father told him that if he wanted
to see his daughter, he must come to the house. 'I had suspicions that
he was not running straight,' he later recalled. News of Bee soon
came. One of May's brothers reported that he had seen Bee, who was

drinking heavily on account of having just lost his job, due to taking a week's unauthorized leave. Her father told her it was as well his true character had come to light before marriage, and told her to break off the engagement and return his presents, which she did, except for the bicycle, which she used to travel to work.

This did not stop Bee from trying to contact her. Her father ignored his three letters to him, asking for permission to see her. However, he could not prevent Bee from meeting her. They met, at least once, on Acton Green, where they had often met in the past. It seems she did not like such attention, but had to talk to Bee in order to avoid a scene. In any case, she wished to thank him properly for the bicycle. She also told him, 'I must ask you not to send anything to Wakefield's, not even letters, for they do not like it', but to direct any letters to her father.

On the evening of Saturday 7 August, May was waiting at the house gates for her parents to return. She had been at work that day, and, because she was helping Wakefield clear a few things up, was later than usual. She had returned home at 8.00. Meanwhile, Bee had been having a rough time of things. He had been working as a journeyman painter, staying at Cromartie House at Park Road North, but had been thrown out because of rent arrears. Afterwards, he had been drinking whisky in a pub on the High Street and then went to Colville Road in search of May. Finding her, he began to talk to her in a hushed voice. Perhaps he was begging her to renew the engagement. She was quiet, too, but one word was heard: 'No'. Mrs Mason, a neighbour, witnessed the scene. A child asked her if Bee was May's father, but was told he was not. 'Is it her chap, then?' 'No, because she doesn't speak to him now.' But what happened next horrified them.

Bee's arms made rapid motions. He had lunged towards May, which seemed, perhaps to onlookers, like a lovers' embrace – but he

Colville Road, Acton, 2005. The author

was holding an open razor. May screamed and tried to run away. Her sister Lillian ran out towards her, just in time to catch the dying girl. Pushing past her and into the house, Bee then took the razor, now covered in blood and turned it on himself. He slashed his own throat and fell to the ground in the front room, groaning before falling unconscious, though only May's youngest sister, Clara, who wrenched the weapon from his hand, paid any attention to him.

May was dying in a pool of her own blood, having had her windpipe severed. Before the doctor or police arrived, she was dead, though no one could have done anything for her. Bee, however, was still breathing and possibly wanted to say something. He was taken to Acton Cottage Hospital, but it was too late for him too. Meanwhile, May's body had not been moved and was examined by Dr Christy of Fairlawn Park. By this time, a large crowd of spectators had arrived, eager to view the corpse. Some of those who did fainted. May's parents returned to this horrific scene at 11.15.

The inquest took place two days later at Acton Fire Station. While the family sobbed, the proceedings began, though as sensitively as possible. May's father had alluded to Bee as being somewhat of a mystery. That mystery was now to be solved. A letter had been received from a certain Alice Bee of Islington. John Bee, it seemed, had been leading a double life. While he appeared to be a respectable young man, this had all been a tissue of lies. Alice Bee had written

> I regret seeing in the paper today the dreadful end of your young daughter. I will appear at the inquest tomorrow, as I think I am John Bee's wife, and mother of his four children. I sympathise with you.

But she could not arrive until later in the day, on account of her having to work. So the identification of the bodies was carried out and witnesses to the murder made their statements. Other evidence was produced. This included a letter by May to Bee, thanking him for the bicycle and arranging to meet him to thank him properly for it. A photograph of May was found on his person. Letters from Bee were read – they begged May 'to have him back'. The weapon was examined. Police and medical evidence was given.

The coroner found the case easy to sum up. He thought that May's father and May herself had acted quite rightly in their behaviour towards Bee after he failed to take her to the seaside. He suggested that the jury bring in a verdict of murder and suicide if they thought that Bee had malice beforehand. The jury agreed and added their sympathy to the family. They also commended the actions of the police in their prompt rendering of first aid to try and save Bee's life.

Acton Cottage Hospital, c.1910. LBE

Finally, Mrs Bee arrived. She was a poor woman, aged 30, her eyes were worn and her hands looked as if they did a great deal of work. She identified the body of her late husband. After leaving the mortuary, she sobbed. Then she told her story. She married Bee in 1895; he was either 34 or 37 at death. His father was a watchmaker from Southwark. In 1903 they separated because of Bee's drinking habits. She had not received any money from him since and had only seen him once more, and that was when he was with another woman. Had Bee wished to marry May, his wife would not have objected. She added that his favourite drink was whisky and when drunk 'he was like a mad man'. Finally, she expressed her shock at the murder, her sympathy for the family and wished to have nothing more to do with her late husband, not even to attend his funeral.

Both funerals took place on 14 August, a week after the murder and suicide. Bee's burial was very quiet and very few attended it. May's was quite the reverse. A service was held in All Saints' Church, South Acton, and then the funeral procession went through packed streets until it reached the cemetery. Thousands witnessed the last journey of May's corpse. A whole host of wreaths were laid by family, friends and employers and colleagues, past and present. Few would forget that day.

Chapter 19

Mad or Bad?
1912

I did not mean to shoot her.
I meant to frighten her.

In 1911, Charles Jones had just published his second book celebrating the achievements of the new Borough of Ealing and its citizenry. Titled *A Decade of Progress* it trumpeted enthusiasm about the local state of affairs. Such optimism probably took a dent in the following year. A century after the murder of Spencer Perceval, there was another murder, but this time it was actually committed in Ealing.

Arthur James Benbow, aged 49 in 1912, and of independent means, seemed harmless, if eccentric. Those who were his acquaintances referred to him as a 'perfect gentleman'. His physical description was as follows: 'Of slight build, and with the stoop of the student, he is of dark sullen, features, has a dark moustache, wears spectacles, and usually, a trilby hat.' He was in the happy circumstances of not needing to work and his innocent amusements were walking around West Ealing and reading, especially books on natural history. The Natural History Museum at Kensington was one of his haunts too. He had lived in Ealing for some years, boarding with a number of households, but never putting down roots anywhere. He was a loner, being a bachelor and lacking any close friends.

Unfortunately he was rather odd in his habits. Some were harmless, if disconcerting; one landlady in Kingsley Avenue stated he never once spoke to her 5-year-old daughter during a sojourn of ten months, always stayed in the bath for an hour in the summer and never let anyone see the contents of his large boxes and trunks which contained his worldly possessions. Most of all, though, he was a hypochondriac, obsessed that he was unwell, despite the protestations of his doctor. Benbow was convinced that he was seriously ill, though his doctor insisted it was only a case of indigestion. At one house that he stayed at, he was convinced that his landlady was attempting to poison him and told his doctor such, only retracting the allegation when he faced

Kingsley Avenue, Ealing, c.1910. LBE

a prosecution for libel. Leaving this house without any warning, he stayed at a house in Hastings Road, where his behaviour became odder. On two occasions he was found by his host to be wandering around inside the house in the very early hours of the morning – once he demanded a doctor to visit him and on the other he removed a fish he thought to be suspicious from the pantry. After both incidents he apologised profusely.

On 13 March 1912, he left his previous lodgings and moved to stay in two rooms in the house of two middle-aged spinster sisters, Misses Sophia and Sarah Baker, who lived in Kingsley Avenue, West Ealing, 'one of its [Ealing's] quietest and most remote residential districts'. The two sisters had recently retired from their millinery business in London. A recurring instance of Benbow's eccentricities was soon noticed: Sarah later said that she had found him, fully dressed, trying the front door at 6.00 in the morning and had been told he was ill. On suggesting he visit a doctor, he refused. Finding him rather eccentric, they said that they would like him to leave. Benbow did not show any signs of anger at this.

The morning of Tuesday 2 April began in an ordinary enough manner: Sarah Baker left the house at 9.00 to do some shopping. Just before she did, she requested that he leave their house. Benbow left at about 10.00 for a stroll, returned and read a newspaper for a while. Sophia asked if he would like breakfast, but he refused. All perfectly normal.

Then matters changed. Benbow went to the kitchen and spoke to Sophia, who was busy making a pudding. He later explained what had happened, and why:

When I went to sleep I had terrible dreams. I thought someone came in and threw something over my head. I thought someone was attending me and had operated upon me. It may be a delusion on my part. I asked her who had performed an operation on me a fortnight ago in the night and she said she knew nothing about it.

When she replied that she did not know what he was talking about, Benbow threatened her with a Colt revolver. The terrified lady still could not answer the question. He then pointed the gun at her and fired point blank. He could not miss. The bullet struck her through the heart and she died instantly. Shocked, Benbow drank a little brandy and then tried to revive his victim with water. When this failed, and not knowing what to do, he thought it best to await the arrival of Sarah. However, he took the precaution of reloading the gun, in case, as he later said, the neighbours tried to lynch him.

The murder was discovered by Sarah at 12.45, though at first, being unable to see the fatal wound, she thought her sister had only fainted. Unable to revive her, she dashed out of the house to summon help. When she informed Benbow of her sister's death, Benbow was silent and motionless. Fortunately a passer-by went to find a doctor and, again fortunately, Dr George Phillips had been attending a patient in the nearby St Stephen's Road. Once he had ascertained what had happened, Phillips stayed with Benbow, who was sitting quietly in a room on the ground floor, while his driver went for the police. Benbow tried to leave the house, but was restrained by Phillips, who held the man's wrists until the police could take charge. Two constables eventually arrived, with inspectors and detectives coming later. Benbow explained 'I am sorry this has happened. I did not mean to shoot her. I meant to frighten her.' He then told the police of the conversation he had had with the deceased. Benbow said his revolver was upstairs, but a search there revealed nothing. When Benbow was searched, his gun was found in his pocket. It was then removed. There was then almost another fatality, because when Inspector Deeks examined the revolver, it exploded in his hand, with a bullet narrowly missing Detective Dobbs's head.

An examination of Benbow's bedroom revealed the following. Under the bed was a tin box. It contained ammunition for the revolver which Benbow used, medical prescriptions, bottles of medicines and tablets. During all this time, Benbow appeared calm. The police took their prisoner to the police station where he was formally charged. Benbow said, 'I object to wilful murder: I did not know it [the revolver] was loaded'. On the way to the police station, Benbow asked an officer to fetch his money from his trunk at the house, a sum amounting to £4.

Benbow appeared before the magistrates at Brentford Police Court on the following morning, charged with the wilful murder of Miss Sophia Baker. Detective Inspector Pike merely wished the court to grant a remand, as the case would have to be tried at the Old Bailey. Benbow made a strange statement, referring to terrible dreams he was experiencing, about someone throwing something over his head and then operating on him. He appeared most puzzled by the turn of events, stating

> *I didn't explain very well. I am so confused just now that I can't give you a proper idea of what the delusion was. I ought to have had expert advice upon it. I have seen a man up town about it. It sounds very mad. It sounds like a case for Broadmoor.*

The court remanded him for a week.

Ealing Town Hall, c.1930. Reg Eden's collection

Brentford Police Court, 2005. The author

On 4 April the inquest was held at Ealing Town Hall by Reginald Kemp, deputy county coroner. Sarah formally identified the body and then related her evidence about finding it. She was pressed with the question that, if she believed Benbow was mad, why had she not taken precautions, but she replied that they had believed him to be harmless. The questioning on this point was so aggressive by one juryman that the man in question had to be asked to leave, which he did, much to his own relief. Dr Phillips related his story and was commended for his courage. The jury were told that the verdict could be manslaughter or accidental death if it was thought that there was no intention to kill or, if intent beforehand could be proved, then they should pronounce it murder. However, the coroner thought that it was intentional as the pistol had been pressed against the victim. The jury concluded that the cause of death was wilful murder whilst of unsound mind. Two days later, Sophia Baker was buried at Marlborough. By the following year, her surviving sister had moved away from Ealing.

After the inquest, the case came up before the magistrates at Brentford again. Sarah and Phillips repeated their evidence, and the police theirs. Exhibits, such as the revolver and the cartridges were displayed. The police surgeon, Dr Bennett, said that he thought Benbow was suffering from delusions about having been operated upon and so was of unsound mind. When he was examined he 'did not appear to understand the seriousness of what had happened, and had the appearance of being mad'. He was then committed for trial at the Old Bailey.

At the Central Criminal Court on 24 April, Benbow was put on trial for murder. It was concluded that he was insane and so not responsible for his actions. Therefore, though he was found guilty, Mr Justice Coleridge ordered that he be detained at His Majesty's pleasure, and he was admitted to Broadmoor Criminal Lunatic Asylum. It is probable that he (like Prince in 1897) was suffering from what would be later termed paranoid schizophrenia. He certainly imagined events which had not occurred and reacted violently against others because of this delusion. Benbow was certainly mentally un-balanced, but he was more fortunate than his victim, Sophia Baker, because he lived for another 34 years, dying in the asylum in 1946.

Chapter 20

The Second Double Tragedy at Acton
1917

A bloody clasp knife was later found in the room.

There were few murders in and around Ealing between the death of Miss Baker in 1912 and that of Sybil Armstrong in 1932. One exception occurred in South Acton, and it resulted in two deaths: that of perpetrator and victim.

The morning of Wednesday 22 August 1917 began as normal for the Fielding family of Clovelly Road, Acton. Thomas Whitehouse Fielding, a 49-year-old canteen porter at the large Acton electrical works, CAV, was in the ground-floor bedroom with his 3-year-old daughter, Doris Violet. He was reading and Doris was asleep. His wife, Mrs Rose Sarah Fielding, was in the scullery, doing some washing. He was not at work because he felt unwell, having been off on the two previous days. He had been unable to eat his breakfast, though he accepted a cup of tea at 6.45 am.

Mrs Fielding, once she had finished her washing, went to the bedroom at about 10 am to find her purse. She was surprised that the door was locked and that, on knocking, she did not receive a reply. She went around to the window and was shocked at the sight which greeted her eyes. Rushing back inside the house, she forced the door (which had been fastened by a chair underneath the door handle) and then the full horror hit her.

Both her husband and youngest daughter were dead. He was on the floor whilst Doris was lying on the bed. Both had had their throats cut. Doris had also been stabbed in the breast. A bloody clasp knife was later found in the room. It was a knife belonging to her husband and which he habitually carried on his person. A medical examination later noted that Fielding had three wounds on his throat; two superficial and one deep. These had been self-inflicted. There were a number of stab wounds to the child's body, as well as the throat wound. All had been caused by the bloody knife.

Clovelly Road, Acton, 2005. The author

Dr Sibley was called for and certified that both were dead. He called for a constable, who duly arrived and noted that there were no signs of any struggle. The corpses were removed to the mortuary and an inquest was held at the Fire Station on Friday 24 August. This was held by Reginald Kemp, Coroner for West Middlesex.

What had happened was clear enough. Fielding had attacked his child, and when she was dead, ended his own life. The question was not whodunnit, but why it had been done. He had four other children and seemed devoted to his family. There was no family history of insanity and there were no money troubles. He had a full-time permanent job, being 'an old servant of the company, and was allowed to work, or not work, pretty much as he liked'. His wife had not noticed anything out of the ordinary in his behaviour. He slept well and never threatened to commit suicide.

It seems that Fielding was ill and feared that he would get worse. He had suffered from pneumonia in December 1916, which had caused him to be absent from work in the early months of 1917. But he had appeared to be quite well in recent months. Although he should have gone for a medical inspection in July, he had failed to do so. A colleague reported that Fielding was 'occasionally depressed' because of his illness. It was thought that he believed that he had the first symptoms of consumption and this had 'affected his brain' and thus he killed Doris while of an unsound mind. Dr Dawe noted that Fielding was suffering from the after-effects of pneumonia and the lungs were not properly cleared; yet there was no sign of tuberculosis.

It is possible that an accident he had had on Sunday 19 August may have had an effect on him. He was travelling to Kew and, while waiting for a tram in Chiswick High Road, he was knocked down by a cyclist. Dismounting, the man asked if Fielding was hurt. Fielding replied in the negative and the two went on their separate ways. However, when Mrs Fielding returned home that evening, she found her husband already in bed. As noted, he did not go to work on the following days. Dawe noted 'tuberculosis sometimes induced a depressed and morbid tendency of the mind and it was also quite possible that the blow received from the fall might have lacerated the brain, and thus affected it'.

The coroner concluded that Fielding had killed his child and then committed suicide. It was up to the jury to decide whether he was of unsound mind, which they duly did. Sympathy was expressed to the widow. This was a tragedy which had happened by mischance. Perhaps, if Fielding had not been knocked over on Sunday, the fragile balance of his mind would have held together and the deaths would not have occurred. Yet, considering his real illness of the recent past and his current medical fears, this accident acted as a catalyst which was to prove fatal.

Chapter 21

Murder at the Hospital 1932

Why you have degraded yourself and brought yourself so low?

On 12 July 1932, four shots were fired in Ealing and Chiswick Isolation Hospital at Pope's Lane, Ealing: a shocking occurrence which was the climax of a tale of love and rage. According to *The Middlesex County Times*, 'Not within living memory had such an appalling tragedy happened in Ealing', though this overlooked the shooting by Arthur Benbow of Sophia Baker only twenty years before, and the killing of Gladys Ruxton in 1915 (not described in this book).

Sybil Armstrong was born in 1909 and had had a comfortable start in life – at least from one point of view. She had had a college education and played the cello and piano. She played in St Helen's Amateur Orchestral Society in Lancashire, as did her father, John. However, from another point of view, her childhood and youth had been unhappy. Her father, a retired tailor and aged 55 in 1932, was a heavy drinker. His wife once described him as being an 'absolute maniac' when he was drunk. He was also very strict and both mother and daughter went in fear of him.

In order to escape the effects of her father's drinking habits, Sybil left the family home in Daulton Street, St Helen's, in 1931. She went down to London and obtained a post in Battersea General Hospital as a nurse. It was whilst she was working there that she fell in love with one of the patients. His name was William Bambrick, an oxy-acetylene worker of Winchester Street, Pimlico. Ellen Parrish, who boarded in the same house as he did, described him as 'a hard working, steady young man'. He was much in love with Sybil, referring to her as 'a good and straightforward girl and both of us had upright and honest intentions'. Sybil's parents only learnt of this association when she returned home for a few weeks in March 1932.

Apart from being a heavy drinker, John Armstrong held strong views on matters of social class. Once he knew of his daughter's

Ealing and Chiswick Isolation Hospital, Pope's Lane, Ealing, 1903. LBE

romance with Bambrick, his rage knew no bounds and he considered him 'to be below his Daughter's Station in Life'. He told her that the two must part and when she refused, his anger grew. Escaping to London, she decided to change her job so her father would not be able to track her down.

She began to work at the Ealing Isolation Hospital on 25 May as a probationer nurse, but unfortunately the matron, Ida Gregory, wrote to her father to inform him of his daughter's whereabouts. Armstrong told Miss Gregory that he wanted to know if his daughter associated with men. Armstrong also found where Bambrick lived and told him not to associate with his daughter. He refused. Armstrong visited Bambrick's mother in Battersea, in his pursuit of his daughter. He insulted her, saying 'My daughter is rich, beautiful and talented and if she could see you she would wipe her feet on your son.' He also threatened her son, saying to his mother, 'I will put something in him.' Coincidentally, he found that Mrs Bambrick was also against any marriage, 'because I felt it might lead to unhappiness'.

Matters came to a head in early July. Sybil and Bambrick became engaged and had their banns read out at St Gabriel's in Pimlico. Sybil was late in returning to the hospital on the evening of 8 July and had to explain to the matron that she had been seeing her fiancé and was shortly to wed. Sybil had to resign and give a month's notice, which she did. She would cease employment at the hospital on 8 August and they planned to go to India after the wedding.

This was not the last of her troubles. Miss Gregory wrote to her father, telling him about the latest developments in the case. He travelled down to Ealing and in the early afternoon on 12 July arrived, unannounced, at the hospital. According to the matron, 'He appeared excited and emotional and very concerned about his daughter's future.' He was sober, but had been drinking, and later a half-empty bottle was found on his person. Sybil was called into the matron's office.

On seeing her father, she was angry and surprised. Armstrong wanted his daughter to return with him. A heated argument then ensued once she refused to leave. Armstrong called Bambrick 'a low person and the son of a charwoman in a brewery'. He made further appeals to his daughter, demanding to know 'Why you have degraded yourself and brought yourself so low?' Sybil replied robustly, with sentences such as 'Don't come near me', 'Don't touch me, you have been drinking' and 'I hate the ground you walk on'. None of which, of course, were likely to appease the angry man. Miss Gregory tried to intervene, by saying 'Don't make a scene – do go with your father'. It had no effect.

It was then that Armstrong must have realized that all means of verbal persuasion were exhausted. He went to his overcoat, which he had hung over a chair, and drew out a Webley revolver. He pointed it at his daughter. Miss Gregory tried to pull his arm down, but was shot in her arm, and she left to fetch help. It was too late. Three shots rang out in quick succession and when Miss Minty, another nurse, arrived, just after 1 o'clock, all she could see were the two corpses. Two bullets were in Sybil's body and one in her father's head. Police and an ambulance were immediately summoned, but were too late. Although both were rushed to the King Edward Memorial Hospital in Ealing, Sybil was already dead and her father expired at 8.50 pm.

An inquest was held on 14 July and Mrs Armstrong identified the bodies. She gave evidence about her late husband's rages and his drinking habits. Apparently she, too, had been threatened by her husband in the past. The police doctor described the fatal wounds and the house surgeon at Ealing hospital gave additional evidence. Because Miss Gregory was still suffering from her injury, the inquest was adjourned until 29 July. On this occasion, the matron was congratulated on her courage in her attempt to stop the crime, although no one noted that, if she had not informed Armstrong of his daughter's romance, the tragedy would never have occurred. In any case, it was a swift and straightforward matter. Evidence of Mr Armstrong's temper was given, and William Bambrick spoke briefly. Miss Gregory gave the most important evidence, as she had been an eyewitness to the argument between father and daughter, and to Armstrong threatening his daughter with a revolver. The jury brought in the only verdict possible – murder followed by suicide.

Chapter 22

He didn't Mean to Do it
1936

I held onto her neck, and
she fell to the floor.

Not all of Britain was equally affected by the Depression of the 1930s. Districts which depended on traditional heavy industry, such as mining and ship-building, were certainly hard hit, with high unemployment. But other districts saw an expansion of industry and employment, such as the Midlands and the south-east of England. New industries sprang up around Perivale and Greenford, attracting workers from the depressed regions.

Alfred George Gilbert and Catherine McLeod had been childhood sweethearts in Wales in the 1920s and early 1930s. Alfred had been employed in the coal-mines, but had been obliged to give up work due to injuries sustained there. Catherine left Wales before Alfred as she wanted to earn money so that they could be married sooner than would otherwise have been the case. She obtained domestic work in a number of households and gave great satisfaction. When Alfred arrived, he worked as a delivery man for the Pitshanger Lane branch of Messrs F S Stowell Ltd, wine merchants. He too did well in his job and was popular with customers.

They were married by licence in St John's Church, West Ealing, by the Revd Summerhayes in November 1934. They then began to live at Conway Crescent in Perivale, on which they were able to take out a mortgage because of the money Alfred had received as compensation for his mining injury. Everything seemed to be going well for the young couple; in 1936, Alfred was 22 and his wife 26. Catherine's brother, who lived nearby, later said that the two were perfectly happy together, and neighbours said the same.

Unfortunately, in February 1936, Alfred was found to have embezzled money, about £4 in all, from his employers by not passing all the money his customers gave him to the manager, Harry Pearcey. It was not the first time this had happened; presumably the earlier offence had been overlooked. On 3 March, Pearcey confronted him

Conway Crescent, Perivale, 1930s. LBE

with this and he did not deny it. Pearcey then said he would have to report this to the head office and that Alfred should go home, suspended from his employment, which he did.

Alfred cycled home, arriving, according to a neighbour, at 10.30 am. Catherine realized that something must be wrong. He told her all. She said that she would see Mrs Pearcey, the manager's wife, and use her savings to repay the money he had taken and so settle the matter. Alfred opposed this plan and the two argued about it. Catherine kept saying she would pay the money back but this only served to antagonize her husband.

Later, Alfred made a statement to the police and described what happened next. He said:

> *I caught hold of her neck with both hands. She cried, 'Darling, please.'*
> *I held onto her neck, and she fell to the floor. I fell with her, and after a*
> *few moments of struggling she lay still. I don't know why this happened*
> *this morning. My wife and I never quarrelled, and I thought she would*
> *be better off than living with a thief.*

For some reason, Alfred then tied a piece of string around her neck. Shortly after 11, a neighbour saw him leaving the house and asked him if he was having a day off, to which he replied in the affirmative. Then he went to a cycle shop in Perivale and asked the owner, Mr Wash, to take him by car to Pitshanger Lane. Wash did so and received 5s. Returning to his place of work, he asked Pearcey if he would telephone the police because he had just killed his wife. Pearcey told him that he should hand himself into the police himself. Before he left the shop, it was noticed that he had blood on his hands, but seemed quite normal otherwise.

At the junction of Montpelier Road and Castlebar Road, Alfred saw a police car. Stopping it, he told them that a murder had been committed and the driver asked him to step inside. Once there, he told them that he had killed his wife. Although cautioned, he went into more details, finally saying, 'Don't let me see her again.' They drove to his home and two policemen investigated.

They found Catherine lying on her back in the scullery. She was fully clothed, and a night-dress and an apron also covered her. When these were removed, string was seen tied around her neck. Despite their attempts, and those of Dr Stewart, they were unable to revive her and concluded she was dead. Dr Weston, the police divisional surgeon, examined the corpse. He concluded that death was due to 'asphyxia by manual strangulation'. There were abrasions around the neck as well as the weal encircling it. The latter was inflicted after death. Inspector Warren arrived just before noon and took Alfred to Greenford Police Station. Here he was told by Divisional Detective

Pitshanger Lane, Ealing, 1970s. Reg Eden's collection

Inspector Thomas that he would probably be charged with murder and Alfred confessed all of what had happened, beginning with the words, 'I just did it. That's all. I will tell you what happened.' He was formally charged with murder that afternoon.

Then the formal mechanics of the law began to roll. Alfred appeared before the magistrates at a special sitting of the Ealing Police Court on the afternoon of 3 March, where he was remanded in custody for a week. Alfred said he did not want any legal help, but was given it nevertheless. Two days later, an inquest was opened at Ealing Town Hall, but, apart from the identification of the corpse by her brother, Andrew McLeod, who also lived on Conway Crescent, the inquest was adjourned indefinitely. The Gilbert home was guarded by the police.

On 10 March, the police case was first heard before a packed court. Alfred's solicitors entered a plea of not guilty, but he exclaimed, 'I done it. He doesn't plead "Not guilty". He pleads "Guilty"'. With that he collapsed and had to be carried out of the dock. After statements made by witnesses, he was committed to trial.

The trial took place nine days later. Alfred was defended by Mr Christmas Humphreys (a former resident of Ealing), who stated that the only verdicts which could be given were manslaughter or murder. As he said, there was no dispute that Alfred had killed his wife. What was to be determined was whether there had been malice beforehand – making all the difference between murder and manslaughter. Alfred was strong and his wife's neck was weak. Little force would have been required to kill her. He reminded the jury that the couple were deeply in love with each other and that he stood to gain nothing from his act against her. He spoke of the killer's 'pathetic futility' and 'stupid pride'. The jury were reminded that Gilbert gained nothing from his wife's death. It was suggested that he was unwell and suffering from 'depression' and so acted in an uncharacteristic manner.

The jury found the accused guilty of manslaughter and he received the sentence of three years' penal servitude. This was extremely lenient. The judge, Mr Justice Hawke, remarked, 'I have with some difficulty persuaded myself to pass the lightest sentence that can be passed on a person sent to penal servitude.' It would appear that Humphreys's brilliant speech had been decisive in gaining the jury's sympathy.

Chapter 23

Murder of his Best Friend
1936

I got the truncheon out of his hands and struck blindly as hard as I could.

Tennis was one of the main props of the social scene in Ealing – and probably throughout middle class England between the two World Wars. George Orwell's anti-hero, George Bowling in *Coming up for Air* is eloquent on this point:

> *I was living in a boarding-house in Ealing. I . . . belonged to a local tennis club. You know those tennis clubs in the genteel suburbs – little wooden pavilions and high wire-netting enclosures where young chaps in rather badly cut white flannels prance up and down, shouting 'Fifteen–forty!' and 'Vantage all!' in voices which are a tolerable imitation of the Upper Crust.*

In 1936, the *Ealing Year Book* noted that there were thirty-six tennis clubs in Ealing. The 1930s were, in a way, the golden age for tennis in England – Fred Perry, himself hailing from Ealing, won the Men's Singles at Wimbledon on three occasions. All this might be seen as an example of snobbery but relatively harmless. Yet that would be a mistake. It was deadly enough in Ealing in 1936.

On Wednesday 5 August 1936, one Linford Derrick went to Ealing Police Station. He had a startling report to make to Detective Inspector William Tarr:

> *I have murdered my best friend, Arthur Earle Wheeler, at Winscombe Crescent. I would naturally like to tell you all about it. He was my best friend – in fact, my only friend here. I will tell you all about it as far as I can remember.*

At the trial, it was commented that this was not an everyday occurrence at Ealing Police Station.

Who was Derrick? Who was Wheeler? How and why had the former killed the latter? Derrick was more than eager to give the police a statement, outlining his version of events.

Linford Derrick was then aged 41, and was a Berkshire County lawn tennis coach. He lived at Lammas Park Road as a boarder. He was described as 'a tall athletic looking man, with intensely blue eyes and graying hair'. Wheeler was a 43-year-old insurance agent who worked in London and had lived in Winscombe Crescent since 1923. He was a family man, married to Kathleen, and they had two young girls. Although reasonably well known in the district, they had few close friends. Their connection with Derrick was because of their mutual interest – tennis – and they played at courts near Pitshanger Lane.

In about 1933, Derrick, who was separated from his wife, became acquainted with the Wheelers. Derrick often visited their house and was on friendly enough terms with them to go on holiday with them to Bognor in 1935. As Wheeler was at work in the daytime, Derrick often saw his wife alone, taking her in his car on shopping trips and to the cinema. This was certainly useful for Mrs Wheeler as the family lacked a car and lived about a mile from Ealing Broadway, the main shopping nexus of the locality.

On 1 August 1936, Kathleen Wheeler and her children were driven by Derrick to Felpham in Sussex for their annual holiday. Wheeler joined them later by train. A happy weekend was apparently spent, before Wheeler had to return to work on 4 August. They would return to Felpham on the following weekend. Wheeler was driven home by Derrick. Not unnaturally, having been taken from his family and having to work, Wheeler was rather morose. In order to lift his spirits, Derrick suggested they have supper together that night. They arranged to meet up at Wheeler's home later that evening.

For what happened next we only have Derrick's word. He had been given a key to Wheeler's house, where he stayed for part of the day, reading, and later bought some food. He then met Wheeler at Ealing Broadway Station in the early evening. They had a couple of drinks at the *Railway Hotel* (destroyed by bombing in 1944) while Wheeler talked about the war, in which both had served, but did not discuss personal matters. It was after 9.00 that they returned to Wheeler's home and ate. Derrick discussed the arrangements for travelling down to Felpham at the weekend. Then the talk became nasty. Wheeler said that he did not want Derrick staying with his family when they were on holiday. A quarrel arose about this matter, 'but I can't remember what was said', Derrick later recalled.

Derrick left at 11.00 and drove home. Once back at his lodgings, Derrick was unable to sleep. Feeling unhappy about what had just passed, he wanted to end the quarrel and so walked to Wheeler's house in the early hours of the morning. Wheeler, wearing pyjamas, let him in. In his hand was a truncheon, a weapon he habitually kept near the front door in case of burglars. Derrick told him that he wanted to patch things up.

The two men walked upstairs, Wheeler claiming he needed to put some clothes on. He was not in a good temper. Passing the bedroom, Wheeler remarked 'I suppose you would like to see yourself in that bed with Kath'. Derrick then graphically recalled the next few dramatic moments thus:

> *I fizzed a bit . . . and then told him he was a swine to say a thing like that. He jumped at me with the truncheon raised, and said something which ended 'You . . . swine'. His face had a terrible expression . . . I ducked and dodged away . . . He aimed a blow at me with the truncheon and I seized his left arm . . . After a few moments I was conscious of what seemed like a horrible clanging of bells. I got the truncheon out of his hands and struck blindly as hard as I could . . . It became a horrible, animal sort of scrap . . . I remember we were both lying on the floor almost all-in. The whole thing was a nightmare . . . I suddenly saw a shirt on the floor . . . I tied the sleeve around his neck and pulled it . . . He suddenly became still and I collapsed on the body.*

After he regained consciousness, Derrick was in a quandary about what to do next. He washed the bloodstains from himself and the truncheon. Then he thought the best solution was to make it look as if there had been an attempted burglary and that Wheeler had been killed by the thief. So he removed all the money he could find in the house and took one of Mrs Wheeler's rings. As his clothes were blood-stained, he changed into one of Wheeler's suits. On returning home, he changed again. He then decided that the staged burglary was a nonsensical idea. After rejecting the idea of ending his life with the aid of a gas tap, he decided to tell all to the police.

How much truth was there in this account? Was Derrick holding something back? In order to discover the truth, the police began their investigation promptly, entering the house by the French windows. Detective Inspector Tarr had seen Wheeler's corpse prior to his initial questioning of Derrick and had noted the broken staircase. Other than these, there was little disarray in the house of death. On Wednesday afternoon at the Wheeler's home, photographs were taken as evidence. Then the house was guarded that night and on Thursday several objects were removed for further examination. Sir Bernard Spilsbury, famed Home Office pathologist, conducted the post-mortem examination.

He stated 'The cause of death, in my opinion, was concussion, due to injuries to the head, accelerated by strangulation by a ligature tied round the neck.' There had been three truncheon blows to the head. It was unclear whether Wheeler had been unconscious prior to death. There was also dispute about the nature of the fight. Compared to Wheeler, Derrick only bore slight injuries; mere scratches on his face. This seemed to contradict Derrick's statement about being attacked and almost killed by Wheeler.

Another discovery also cast doubt on Derrick's story. Bloodstains and other marks on the staircase were analysed. The conclusion was that someone had walked downstairs in stockinged feet, and then had taken off the socks and put shoes on again. Derrick's bloody clothes included bloody socks, but his shoes were very little marked with blood. The inference was that Derrick's story about being let in was a pack of lies and that he might have let himself in with the key he had been given, removed his shoes and then crept upstairs.

Numerous witnesses were questioned and subsequently testified in court. Although it would appear from Derrick's testimony that Wheeler was jealous of his friendship with his wife, Kathleen denied this. She believed that the two men were good friends and had never rowed, though she made the qualified comment 'they appeared to be on quite good terms'. Yet, according to Derrick, she had told him that Wheeler was jealous of him when he got into one of his moods, which chiefly concerned his work worries. Derrick said that their friendship was perfectly innocent. Even if this was all true, and there is no evidence to the contrary, a jealous man does not need proof for suspecting anyone, even a good friend, of either committing adultery with his wife or at least desiring to do so.

Derrick's arrival at Wheeler's home at 9.00 and his departure at 11.00 were verified by neighbours. One also said they heard noises in the house in the early hours of the morning, and an investigation noted that no lights had been turned on inside the house. A man was seen leaving the house in the early morning, too. A neighbour found that no one answered the door and that the French windows were ajar at 7.50 am on the following day.

It was clear that Derrick had visited Wheeler for dinner, but had returned in the early hours of the morning. He had then killed him and left the house. The question was why he had killed him. Was it premeditated murder? If not, was he acting in self-defence and, if so, was reasonable force used? Derrick's counsel argued that there was no murder case to answer, only manslaughter. However, Derrick was remanded for trial for the murder of Wheeler.

The trial at the Old Bailey took place on 22–23 September before Justice Greaves Lord. Messrs Roberts, Hawke and Bushwell presented the case for the prosecution, whilst Messrs Cassell and Caswell

Winscombe Crescent, Ealing, c.1910. LBE

conducted the defence. Derrick pleaded not guilty to the murder of Wheeler. The case for the prosecution was that Wheeler was jealous of Derrick and the two men fought – with the result that Derrick confessed his guilt to the police. The defence argued that there was no cause for jealousy and that Derrick was a good friend of the family.

The prosecution laid much weight on Derrick's confession to the police that 'I have murdered my best friend'. They argued that Derrick had not killed Wheeler in self-defence, but had viciously struck him when he was on the ground – none of the bloodstains on the wall were higher than 3 feet. In any case, there was no evidence that there had been the fierce struggle which Derrick claimed.

Furthermore, the prosecution argued that Derrick was bent on murder by the fact that he chose to walk the 20 minutes to Wheeler's house rather than take his car, as cars can be easily identified. It was suggested that Derrick then used his key to open the door and took the truncheon that was hanging up behind it. He removed his shoes, quietly ascended the stairs, and attacked Wheeler. He then descended the stairs in his now bloody stockinged feet, which made a clear trail. There was no evidence that Wheeler ever struck Derrick with the truncheon as he bore no injuries of that type. Self-defence was no adequate defence for the killing of Wheeler, they argued, as six blows had been inflicted on Wheeler, not just the one needed to render him hors de combat.

Derrick was put in the dock as a witness in his own defence. He briefly recounted his life story: born in the Malay States in 1894 and brought up in England, he went to public school and fought in the First World War. He married a woman ten years his senior in India. Despite having two sons, they separated in 1930. Since leaving the Army, he had taken various jobs at home and abroad until he became a tennis coach in 1934. He recounted his friendship with the Wheelers, claiming to have been almost one of the family. He told how Kathleen thought her husband was jealous of his friendship with her, but that he had not been told the same by Wheeler. He also told his version of events on 4–5 August. Witnesses spoke of his good character. Charles Hollanby highly commended Derrick's coaching abilities and said, 'All reports from the various clubs were excellent and he appeared to be the perfect gentleman.'

Derrick was then cross-examined. He denied any improper conduct with Kathleen. He also said that he did not take off his shoes at the foot of the stairs, but that he had had time to remove his shoes in a pause during the fight, not using that time to try and escape, because he was in a panic. The prosecution case suggested it was odd that Derrick returned to Wheeler's house at night. If he had wanted to clear matters up, why had he not waited until the next day? It was also noted that he was in good physical condition, compared to the relatively sedentary Wheeler. The defence argued that Derrick believed he was fighting for his life and so behaved in such a deadly manner. The jury were reminded that reasonable force was legal in acting in self-defence. If the jury believed that he acted in such a light, the only charge could be manslaughter.

The jury took an hour and a quarter before reaching their decision. They found Derrick not guilty of murder, but guilty of manslaughter. On the following day, Derrick was sentenced to ten years' penal servitude. The judge thought the jury had 'taken an extremely merciful view'. In his opinion, the killing of Wheeler 'is as near to murder as it is possible to be without actually going over the line which divides manslaughter from murder' and that such a mild verdict would not have been passed a few years before. The difference between the injuries of the two men – the almost physically unscathed Derrick and the battered Wheeler – was said to be evidence of the former's 'animal cruelty and disregard for humanity'.

What had happened at Wheeler's home in the early hours of 5 August will never be completely known. Whether Derrick deliberately murdered Wheeler, or whether he was attacked by him, is unclear. Yet Derrick's vicious attack or counter-attack was brutal. Perhaps he was really in a state of panic, perhaps not, but it was up to the prosecution to convince the jury that he was guilty of murder, and this they failed to do. Derrick was a fortunate man, if nothing else.

Perhaps we should let Agatha Christie (who often visited her grandmother, Mrs Miller, an Ealing resident, on whom the fictional Miss Marple was based) have last word. In one of her novels, published some years after this murder, the protagonist is a professional tennis player with psychopathic tendencies. Coincidence?

Chapter 24

Murder in Southall
1938

The person who committed this
murder was a paltry thief, in need
of warmth and shelter.

Those who know Southall now may not be surprised to learn that in 1934 a book about Middlesex commented that Southall's streets were thronged with immigrants – but these were from Wales, not from India or Somalia (to name but two countries) as in more recent years. Then, as now, the immigrants had arrived in Southall in search of a better life than in their homeland, coming to a place where work was there for the taking. The depression of the 1930s had hit the coalfields in south Wales hard and many people, especially unmarried young men, preferred to take their chances elsewhere and took the train eastwards. One of these men who arrived to work in Southall was not so lucky and this is his story.

Frederick Henry Priddle was born in 1913 in Thomastown, Glamorgan, where his father was a coal miner. He first came to London as part of the government's transfer scheme and undertook training in acetylene welding at Park Royal. He then worked at the Woolf Rubber Factory from 1933 to 1936, at Cricklewood and then Hayes. Falling ill, he left the job and returned home. Once he had recovered, he worked in a colliery for three months, but then fell ill again. Since April 1937 he had been employed at L Clarke and Co., engineers and welders of Acme Works, Pluckington Place, Southall. His employers described him as 'a conscientious and capable workman'.

Priddle was an inoffensive figure, described as a 'very quiet and reserved young man, who did not mix with a lot of people, but kept to the company of a few childhood friends'. He was a teetotaller and rarely went out. When he lived in Wales he was interested in first aid and was a member of the St John's Ambulance Brigade. He had been engaged to Miss Eunice Wiggins (also from Wales) since 1934, and they had known each other for three years before that. She had lived

Southall Railway Station, c.1905. Reg Eden's collection

in Southall from February 1937, keeping house for her brother, following the death of his wife. Priddle often spent his evenings with the two of them or took his fiancée to one of the four cinemas in Southall. Now that Priddle had a settled job, they were hoping to marry soon, but had as yet made no fixed plans.

On 31 December 1937, Priddle and Miss Wiggins went to a New Year's Eve party held at a house of a fellow Welshman in Portland Road, Southall. They played party games and enjoyed themselves there. Miss Wiggins had her fortune told by another guest. She said, 'I was going to hear of a broken engagement' and that 'I should hear of an illness and be sent for quickly to someone's bedside'. It could be argued that all these three events are fairly commonplace and can be predicted without difficulty. Yet they were to come true rather more quickly and tragically than anyone could foresee. Miss Wiggins concluded, 'I had the impression that it was meant to refer to an elderly person living a long way away.'

The engaged couple left the party at 12.35 in the morning. Priddle escorted his fiancée to her home in the Crescent, and then went home himself. He stopped off at the coffee bar on Station Bridge before arriving at his lodgings at Gordon Road. At about 1.30, he was found slumped over the garden gate by his landlord, David Walker, and Ethel, his wife. They had been awoken by groanings and then a loud

Gordon Road, Southall, 2005. The author

noise downstairs and, looking out of the window, saw him there. Mrs Walker urged her husband to investigate. He went downstairs and said to Priddle, 'Come on, old son, what is the matter with you?' Then they saw that blood was flowing from his chest where he had been stabbed. He called his wife down.

Once they had helped him inside, they called for the police and took him to Southall Hospital in an ambulance. It was soon ascertained that, apart from the chest wound, he had been stabbed in the head and kicked in the stomach. The chest wound was 4 inches deep and had been inflicted by a stiletto. No weapon, however, was found at the scene.

The police kept a watch by his bedside. Priddle did regain some consciousness. In brief, disconnected statements, he told them the following in whispers. He had entered the living room in the dark and saw the figure of a man of medium build by the firelight. He was then kicked in the stomach, felt a stab and fell unconscious. After that he had staggered out to the front gate, where he had been found. No one living in this quiet back street had seen or heard anything suspicious.

What was the motive? A box of matches had been broken into and two boxes taken. About 8s and 6d, which had been on the mantelpiece, was missing. An electric light bulb had been removed. The police theory was that two young men who were sleeping rough in the locality were responsible. They were known to carry out the following type of burglary. They would break into premises late at night and take any money or valuables. Then they would make themselves comfortable, have a meal and put coals on the fire, but first would remove the electric light in case of their being disturbed. The police made enquiries in Southall and its environs for these men.

Priddle died at 3.30 in the morning of 14 January. There had been hopes of his recovery, but pneumonia and the loss of blood fatally worsened his condition. Miss Wiggins and his mother were at his bedside. His father had had to return home to work and, although summoned back, he arrived too late. It was now a case of murder. The police had lost the only witness. Divisional Detective Inspector Baker and his men redoubled their efforts and questioned the two men suspected of the crime. They had to be released due to lack of evidence or witnesses. An additional clue was that a car was heard pulling up at the house on the night of the attack, and that a tall, dark man was seen fleeing the scene.

A post-mortem examination was undertaken by Dr Broadridge, the police surgeon. It was hoped that a particle of the murder weapon might be found. None was. Then the inquest was held at St John's Hall on 17 January, but after Priddle's uncle gave formal identification of the body, it was adjourned until 8 February in order to give the police more time for their enquiries.

There was much local sympathy for Priddle's parents, who were living in poor circumstances and had a large family. Local people, 156 in all, from neighbouring streets, gave £4. 7s 3d on his behalf. His workmates and employers also made a collection and sent a wreath to the funeral, which was held on 19 January in Wales. Priddle's parents wrote to express their thanks to the people of Southall for their sympathy and help.

The adjourned inquest was held on 8 February, as planned. Reginald Kemp, the West Middlesex Coroner, observed at the outset that the police 'have an extraordinarily difficult task before them because there is very little for them to go on'. Very little that was new emerged. Miss Wiggins told that Priddle had no worries or any enemies. Frank Mortimer, proprietor of the coffee stall at the railway station, said Priddle was cheerful and well, though quiet, as usual, and left at about 1.20, hoping to catch a bus, but on being told there were none, said, 'All right, I'll have to hoof it.' His landlady made similar remarks.

Her husband said that his theory was that Priddle had been attacked on the way home, but admitted that such was only a theory.

The only question was how did the burglars break in? There was no sign of forced entry and all the doors were locked. Perhaps someone had forgotten to lock the front door. There was also the question of suicide, but this was quickly discarded because no weapon was found, money was missing and Priddle was a contented man. The verdict was wilful murder by person or persons unknown, but with so little evidence, the police could not pinpoint the guilty party. The coroner appealed for anyone with information to come forward. Yet the mystery remained unsolved.

Almost forty years later, the local newspaper ran a feature on the crime, based on an interview with Mr Walker, then aged 89, who still lived at the same house. Nothing new emerged, however, as only cold embers were raked over. The suggestion was made that there were police archives which might shed new light on the case. The murder file became a public document in 1994 but, though it contained information which was not public hitherto, it did not point to a murderer. It is, however, worth examining the additional material.

Priddle, a well-known teetotaller, had had three glasses of wine or beer at the New Year's party, but was not thought to be drunk, his fiancée testifying to his sobriety when they left the party. The description by Priddle of his assailant was as follows, 'wearing a light coat and a cap and was about 5 foot 8 inches'. This could have fitted thousands of men, so was of little use.

Some suspected his landlord as having killed him, but there was no real evidence for such a supposition. Priddle was questioned on this point, but refuted it as a possibility. Other suspects were questioned. One Edward Hooper, a Scot and an army deserter, had a track record of breaking into houses for shelter. On 25/26 December, he had been in a house in Hanger Lane, Ealing, but he could prove he was breaking into St Luke's Vicarage, Hammersmith, on the night of Priddle's assault. Another suspect was Llewellyn Davis, a well-known housebreaker, but he had an alibi, too, for the night in question.

Witnesses gave evidence about acquaintances, lodgers and strangers whose movements on the night of 31 December/1 January could not be accounted for. People who had had blood on their clothes were reported, and there was a reference to a man replying, 'Some people deserve all they get', on being told of Priddle's murder. A newsagent recalled being asked by a man from another part of London to be sent local newspapers just after the crime. A Mr Knight from Salisbury wrote to the police to tell them of a man from Lewisham whom he knew in 1929, and who possessed a stiletto. William Triffit, who was in gaol, told of an acquaintance in

Winchester who committed housebreaking offences and carried a stiletto, but this man turned out to be a mere invention.

The mystery remains unsolved to this day. It seems likely it will remain so. All that can be said is that the attack was probably not based on any personal motive – and so all the more difficult to solve. The police theory of unknown burglars who reacted violently seems probable. As one policeman at the time said

> *the person who committed this murder was a paltry thief, in need of warmth and shelter, and by the ferocity of his assault upon the unfortunate man, is, in all probability, youthful and inexperienced in crime.*

Inspector Baker's concluding report to his superintendent on 5 October 1938, seems appropriate:

> *Despite every possible enquiry and constant touch being kept with persons likely to be able to assist us in this difficult case, no progress has been made. In the event of any useful information coming to hand, it will at once be acted upon and a further report submitted.*

Chapter 25

Led Down the Garden Path
1941

*I am definitely of the opinion that
the cause of death in both cases
was poisoning.*

lthough by the spring of 1941, the Blitz had come to an end,
Mrs Lilian Bounds, a widow, was a worried and a puzzled
woman. She resided in Goring Way, Greenford, 'a road
on the recently built West Ridge Estate, behind Greenford Parish
Church'. The cause for her concern was that she had not seen Phyllis
Elizabeth Crocker, a neighbour and friend of hers, for a few days.
They used to have tea together every day, and communicated at other
times by knocking the ceiling with a broom handle. Mrs Bounds
described her friend as 'bright, jolly, a good companion and an
exceptionally nice woman'.

Phyllis had moved to Greenford in early 1940 with Eileen, her new
baby daughter. She was, at first, a 27-year-old single mother – a rare
phenomenon – and her mother had accompanied her. The elder Mrs
Crocker died in November of that year after a trip to Scotland. In her
stead came one Lionel Rupert Watson, aged 31, a bakelite moulder,

Goring Way, Greenford, 2005. The author

Hoover factory, Perivale, 1939. LBE

who told her he had been married but was now divorced. They had met whilst working together at the Hoover factory in Perivale. The two were married bigamously in January 1941 at Ealing Registry Office and seemed a happy couple. Although Phyllis was a friend of Mrs Bounds, she kept herself to herself as regards the other neighbours, perhaps because her child was illegitimate.

Mrs Bounds had been used to seeing her everyday, but the last time she had seen her was in the garden on the morning of 20 May. Another neighbour, one Mrs Rose Burgess, saw Phyllis and her husband hanging up a sheet on the same day. Both seemed cheerful. Mrs Bounds did not see Phyllis on the following day, as she would have expected. Instead, her husband came around at night and gave her some marrow seeds and a pint of milk which he told her he did not need. Mrs Bounds asked where his wife was. Turning a little pale, he replied, 'She has gone away to her aunt in Scotland.' When Mrs Bounds replied that it was strange that she had not said goodbye, he said that his wife left very early and was in a hurry.

The good neighbour was probably unconvinced. On the following day, she noticed Watson scrubbing and brushing. The pungent smell of disinfectant was in the air. The next day she asked if Watson had heard anything from his wife, and he answered in the negative. On another day he stated that his wife did not want to hear from anyone and this rather upset Mrs Bounds. It was then noticed that a large box which had been in the garden was there no longer, though it was to reappear three weeks later.

To conclude the strange events of May, Watson was seen digging in his garden on 26 May. Mrs Bounds noticed that he was digging beneath the flagstones of the garden path and cheerfully observed, 'Hullo! What are you doing? Are you digging for victory?' Watson replied 'I am going to bury some of this rubbish' and pointed to a sack of cabbage leaves and other debris, which was nearby.

Little of note occurred for the next few weeks. On about 26 June, Mrs Bounds saw Watson watering his garden with a hose and sluicing down the flagstones with disinfectant. There was a stronger smell on the following day and by 30 June it was foul. Enlisting the help of a neighbour, Mrs Bounds investigated. They could, at first, find no sign of the cause of the offensive odour. That evening, the stench was almost unbearable. The indomitable Mrs Bounds armed herself with a chopper and went into her neighbour's garden and removed some of the flagging. What she found was shocking,

The earth beneath was mixed with garden lime, and in it Mrs Bounds felt something soft. She put back the flagstone and went to the police with Mr Burgess.

Police officers duly returned with them and found the bodies of a woman and child beneath the flagstones of the path in the back garden of the maisonette. The woman was lying on her back with her hands crossed and was dressed only in a vest and camisole. The child wore a vest, nightdress and napkin.

On the morning of the following day, Divisional Detective Inspectors Deighton and Smith paid a visit to the factory where Watson was employed. The former told him, 'We are police officers. I am making enquiries respecting the death of your wife and child.' Watson seemed unperturbed by their arrival, 'I know. Don't show me up here. There is no need to hold me. I found them dead Let's go in there [the timekeeper's office].'

Deighton explained that he had seen the bodies at Greenford Police Station on the previous evening and that he was going to take Watson to the station and detain him there. After cautioning him, Watson seemed as unruffled as ever, 'Yes, I know. I found them both dead. I will tell you how it happened later on at the station.' Once there, he stated emphatically 'I did not murder my wife and child.'

On 2 July Watson was charged at Ealing Police Court with the murder of Phyllis and Eileen Crocker. Watson was described at this juncture as 'a well built, dark haired man ... in a blue open necked shirt and a navy pin striped suit. He was unshaven.' Lady Humphreys, the chairman of the bench, asked Watson if he had any questions at this stage. He had not. But he did ask for free legal aid, which was

Greenford Police Station, 2005. The author

granted. The police asked that the prisoner be remanded for a week, which was also granted.

Watson did not have much longer to wait to learn his fate. Mr Morgan opened the case against him, and he called on Mrs Bounds as his leading witness. Once she had related her story, Watson began with his. He explained that Phyllis's mother tried to commit suicide and later died at Isleworth Hospital. Soon afterwards, he and Phyllis learnt that she was pregnant with his child, and they aborted it. He then revealed himself to have been a bigamist. Although he had stated that he was divorced, this was a lie. His real wife was living in Cowgate Road, Greenford, with another man. He added that by the spring of 1941, Phyllis was ill and that she told him she was about to have another baby, but that the doctor disagreed.

On 20 May, the day that Mrs Bounds had last seen Phyllis, Watson suggested to her that they take a walk. According to Watson, she felt unwell, and said she would go to bed. Watson went to see a film at the Granada Cinema. He said:

When I came home, I found her lying dead, on her back. She had been sick. I went into the bedroom and found the baby also dead. I covered the baby and put Phyllis by her.

He spent a restless night. The following day he went to work and in the evening he dug a hole in the garden, put the bodies in and filled it up with earth.

The prosecution ridiculed the story. Morgan claimed it was, 'absolutely incredible'. He found it impossible to believe that Watson did nothing on finding his wife's body; calling neither the neighbours nor a doctor. He must have been making his story up.

It was now time to examine the medical evidence. Sir Bernard Spilsbury, once again in Ealing (see chapter 23), had performed the examination. Since there were no marks on the body and no sign of any disease, he naturally suspected poison. He took organs from Phyllis's corpse and had them presented to Dr Roche Lynch, a Home Office analyst. Lynch told the court:

I am definitely of the opinion that the cause of death in both cases was poisoning by cyanide, and in expressing this opinion I have taken into consideration the important fact that after death cyanide disperses from the body quickly.

Because of this, since his examination was taking place weeks after death, the fact that there were any traces at all meant that a high dosage must have been administered. Spilsbury agreed with this assessment.

A fellow workman at the factory where Watson was employed recalled a discussion about poison between him and Watson in late April or May. Watson asked, 'Can you give me some of your wife's poison tablets?' On being asked why he wanted them, Watson replied, 'I have a dog I want to kill.' His colleague then said that the tablets would be of no use for that, as they were only sleeping pills. But next door to the factory was a shop in which sodium cyanide was regularly used for industrial purposes. Although security precautions were taken, these were not infallible. Other employees mentioned that they had seen Watson handling a lump of (to them) unknown material and Watson explained to them that it was 'some stuff to kill insects in the garden' and to another that it was to clean the bath. The prosecution alleged that this substance was cyanide and it was used to kill his wife. It was suggested that, as cyanide has an obnoxious taste, Watson may have convinced his wife that it was a way of aborting her child.

The motive was said to be Watson's friendship with another female factory employee, Miss Joan Filby, aged 17. After 20 May, the date of the assumed death of Phyllis and Eileen, Watson renewed his association with Miss Filby. This would have been odd if Watson was really griefstricken for his late wife. On 21 May he invited her to go out with him on Whit Monday, and though she did not, they went to the cinema together and he gave her clothes that once belonged to his wife. Although Watson denied any strong feelings for the girl, or any intimacy, a note from him to her was read out in court:

Well, dear, I expect you wonder why I preferred you out of all girls. I have begun to love you and even if you have a boy friend, perhaps there is room for me somewhere. Goodbye, with love. Kisses.

Another witness was Reginald Odell, a bakery delivery man, who said that Watson told him on the early afternoon of 20 May, 'Don't deliver any more. We shan't want it. She is going away.'

The inquest was held at Hayes Town Hall. The West Middlesex Coroner, Mr Broadbridge, announced that investigations into the deaths were still incomplete and that he would have to adjourn the proceedings. However, in order that the corpses could be buried, he did allow them to be formally identified. This was the unpleasant task of Mrs Maud Watson, mother of the accused man. She did so, but said that she did not know Phyllis well, having only met her once, but that she had seen the baby several times in the company of her son.

Meanwhile, the hearing against Watson continued, and this time it was Mr Pierron, for the defence, who was speaking and examining the witnesses. There was some suggestion that the cyanide was to be used to kill the household dog, but there was no corroborating evidence. Questioning Mrs Bounds and Mrs Burgess, it was established that Phyllis had been ill in early 1941 and had spent some time in hospital. This was because she had had a miscarriage.

Dr Thomas Stewart had been Phyllis's doctor. He gave evidence, confirming that he had treated her for influenza in early 1940 and, later, for a septic abortion. She had not consulted him about another pregnancy and he said she seemed to be getting better when he last saw her on 26 April. Yet she was three months pregnant at the time of her death. Watson was committed for trial to the final court.

The trial at the Old Bailey lasted for four days in September. The circumstantial evidence against Watson was strong. Evidence of his interest and possession of cyanide came from some of his workmates. Mrs Bounds gave evidence about Phyllis's disappearance. Joan Filby told of Watson's friendship and 'advances' towards her. Watson stood in the witness box and denied everything with which he had been charged. He said that 'I was passionately fond of Eileen. We were quite happy together.' He admitted taking cyanide to deal with insects and to clean the lavatory, but that was all. He said that he did not alert the police when he claimed to have found the corpses because

I was very upset and in a bit of a fix because I had bigamously married her. Could not call a doctor owing to that. I thought of my children, my job and my people.

Despite the advocacy of Messrs Valetta and Durand for the defence, the jury disbelieved his story and found him guilty and when Mr Justice Cassels passed the death sentence, he added, 'Upon overwhelming evidence the jury have rightly found you guilty of murder.'

Inspector Deighton said of Watson, 'He created a bad impression on the Jury by his callous manner and the way he answered questions.'

Watson, however, maintained his innocence even after the verdict had been passed. He wrote to the Thomases and Burgesses in this vein. Commenting on the principal witness for the prosecution, he wrote of 'things that would prick Mrs Bound's conscience after the way she gave her evidence, some was true and some not'. He added, 'know doubt she thinks I'm a very wickit man for doing what I do do and marrying her like I did'. Finally he added 'I'm not afraid to die I would have gone with Phyllis then if it had not been for my four little children God bless them all.' He attempted an appeal on the grounds of insanity in the family. His great-grandmother died in an asylum in 1912 and his grandmother likewise in 1928. In 1934, his uncle had died of 'general paralysis of the insane and syphilitic aortitis'. Yet the appeal was turned down.

Watson was hanged at Pentonville Prison on 12 November 1941. He was the first man – but as we shall see, not the last – to have been committed from Ealing Police Court to the Old Bailey and to be then sentenced to death. Deighton described the case as 'This fiendish double murder' and said that it had been 'a gruesome job throughout'. The local newspaper added a postscript:

> *He belonged in his small way to that class of murderers – it includes Crippen, Landru and Armstrong – whose cruelty is of such a cold-blooded nature that it alienates any vestige of sympathy from anyone.*

Chapter 26

The Death of a Wanton Woman 1941

The deceased was a woman of immoral character, who has provoked her husband for many years.

For murders 1941 was a grim year in Ealing and Acton. Watson and Ward (see the following chapter) were bad and mad enough, but this murder was viewed rather differently – at least the killer was, because of the differing morals of his victim and himself. It was also another of the stream of domestic crimes chronicled here.

William Alfred Deane and Nancy Helen Holden were a young couple who married at Acton's Catholic church in the summer of 1930 after a whirlwind romance – perhaps because a baby was on its way. Their first child was born in November 1930 and was joined by another in the following year. At this time they lived at a variety of addresses; first in West Ealing, then Twickenham, then settled at Churchfield Road, Acton. The stage, however, was not set for domestic bliss. Quite the reverse, in fact.

Deane drove vans for a living, but was fined for dangerous driving. In 1932, he spent a month in prison for non-payment of the fine. On his release, he discovered that his wife had been 'going about with other men'. She denied it. He resumed driving for a living, this time for Smith & Ward, an Acton firm, working all hours. In 1933, his wife had a miscarriage and a row broke out when he claimed that the child that would have been born was not his. His wife then left him and it was not until the next year that he found her – in Hounslow, working as a prostitute. Yet they resumed living together, first in Chiswick and then in Acton again, at Newton Avenue. She began to work at the Firestone Factory on the Great West Road on shift work, but it was believed that she was still walking the streets.

Newton Avenue, Acton, 2005. The author

The two lived together uneasily for the rest of the decade. It was events in the early years of the Second World War which brought matters to a head. Nancy began to work at the Ultra Radio Co. on the Western Avenue. The children were evacuated to Dawlish, Devon. Nancy began an affair with a fellow employee, Charles Bilby of Chiswick, in 1941. It is not certain when her husband first became aware of this liaison; certainly by July of that year.

In early August 1941, the Deanes went to Devon to visit their children. Nancy returned home first and met her sister, Mrs Violet Gray, the latter's husband, and Bilby at the Railway Tavern in South Acton. Mrs Gray later recalled that Nancy and Bilby had an intimate chat together. A few days later, Deane returned from Devon and went to a pub where he had arranged to meet Nancy. She was not there. So he returned home, and then went out again, returning home at 10.30. His wife was still not back. She did not return until 2 am. Nancy told him that, while he had been in Devon, she had been living with Bilby as man and wife, and was eager to leave him for her lover. Deane then struck her.

Mrs Gray visited her sister on the following day and saw her injury. Nancy told her, 'Look what he has done'. Mrs Gray, replied 'What's happened now?' Deane answered,

She didn't come in until between 1.30 and 2 o'clock. I had been walking the rooms waiting for her to come in. I heard the front gate go, looked out of the window, and saw her in another fellow's arms. She came upstairs and we quarrelled; and that's when I did what I did.

Matters moved to a climax in the following weeks. Bilby called shortly afterwards to ask Deane to let his wife live with him. Deane refused. A week later, there was an anonymous telephone call to Deane's work place. The caller told him that Bilby was at his house every time that Deane was working the night shift. Deane rushed home and found the adulterous couple together. Bilby claimed he was merely bringing a picture frame around. On another occasion, all three were in a pub in Hammersmith and Bilby kissed Nancy. For this, Deane pushed him. He later pleaded with Nancy to leave Bilby, but she refused. At another time, she threw a fork at her husband and later told her sister that she wished it had killed him.

The climax came on the evening of Saturday 3 October 1941. Deane returned home early and was surprised to find his wife preparing to go out. Instead, they had dinner and then Deane read a book. But his wife was determined to go out and issued an ultimatum, 'If you aren't going to take me out, I will go out on my own.' Deane replied, 'Alright, I'll take you out.' They spent a couple of hours at The Six Bells on Acton High Street. They discussed the following day. They were planning to see her father in Twickenham, but Nancy wanted to meet Bilby in the evening.

The argument continued in the kitchen when they arrived home at about 11.00. Deane said, 'I am not going to have him in the house anymore.' His wife replied, 'Whilst I stay here the house is as much mine as yours.' She then said, 'You have made me make up my mind to leave you sooner than I intended.' Deane flew into a rage and his hand fell upon a bowl in which lay a toolmaker's file, which he grasped. He stabbed her with it several times, later recalling, 'I can't remember how many times I stabbed her.' She screamed and then Deane ran out of the house.

Arriving at his father's house in the nearby Clovelly Road, he told him, 'I think I have killed Nancy. She taunted me about going out with another man and I tried to stop her.' He was very distressed and his father went out to call for the police and an ambulance. The two men then went back to the scene of the crime. They found Nancy in the kitchen, where she had fallen. She was covered in blood and moaning. On seeing her husband, she said, 'Go away, I hate you' and 'I am tired, my legs ache'. Police sergeant Newport arrived soon afterwards and Deane told him, 'I have stabbed my wife with a piece of metal. She told me she was going out with another man.' Nancy died later that night. Deane was charged with her murder and Sir

Bernard Spilsbury reported that she had died due to a haemorrhage caused by a stab wound penetrating the heart.

After appearing before Acton Petty Sessions on 4 October and being remanded in custody thereafter, Deane was tried for murder in November. He pleaded guilty. There was a great deal of sympathy for him, even from the relatives of his late wife. George Holden, her brother, said, 'he has been everything a husband could be. He has given her everything she asked for. She slept with other men when he was on night shift.' Mrs Gray added Deane had been 'a wonderful husband to her and I feel sorry for him'. Even the police report concluded, 'there can be no doubt that the deceased was a woman of immoral character, who has provoked her husband for many years'. The only one with a good word for Nancy was Bilby, who said, 'we were very much in love'.

The jury found Deane guilty of murder, but strongly recommended that mercy be shown, because of the provocation he had been sub-jected to and because the killing was not premeditated. His counsel recommended that there should be a retrial because Deane should not have pleaded guilty and because of this the jury was predisposed to find him guilty. This was ruled out of court and so Deane faced the death sentence.

It was no matter that he bore an excellent character and his wife a foul one. The law has to protect all, regardless of their morals. Deane had killed his wife, when all was said and done. Even so, petitions came in, supporting him and asking that his life be spared. On 22 December, Police Commissioner Manwell wrote of the decision to 'respite the capital sentence with a view to its commutation to penal servitude for life'. Deane's life had been saved.

Chapter 27

A Mass Murderer in Ealing 1941

I can't fight millions of people. Therefore, a few must suffer.

aling's history cannot 'boast' of a mass killer on the scale of Jack the Ripper or Reginald Christie. But on 11 November 1941 a number of murders took place in and around Ealing, though these seem to have been quickly forgotten. It was all over quickly enough, but the blood-letting had been on an unprecedented scale – both before and since – and in such a short time. The speed and ferocity are rare for England, but perhaps less so in the USA. Curiously, the case has never been chronicled in print.

It all began in Chiswick on the early morning of Tuesday 11 November. Leslie Ludford, a young solicitor, was buying a poppy on Hadley Gardens, at about 8.50, when a motorist stopped his car nearby and got out. He was armed with a double-barrelled shotgun and fired at Ludford, who tried to escape by entering a nearby garden, but was shot again. He died in hospital shortly afterwards, with three bullets in him. Before he died, he whispered 'Brent. It was Brent.' A witness, Mrs Violet Pinder, was also shot at, but she luckily escaped with her life. Meanwhile, the motorist had driven away. Unbeknown to him, one Mrs Mott had witnessed the scene and ran for help. At 9.20, armed police began their search for the killer.

His next port of call was at St Mary's Grove, also in Chiswick. This was where, at 9 o'clock, he found his next two victims: Mrs Emily Crisp and Mrs Annie New, who lived at Mrs Phyllis Simmond's house (Mrs New was the daughter of Mrs Simmonds). He knocked on the door to summon them, before opening fire. Fortunately, Mrs New was not seriously hurt, but her friend was killed. Kathleen Guyner was next to be shot, this time in Hammersmith, but her injury was not fatal.

He then sped off into Bollo Lane, Acton. Pulling up outside a café, at 9.15, he shot at at Mrs Henrietta Sell, who was out doing her shopping. The killer then drove away at speed, pursued by a lorry.

Level crossing, Bollo Lane, Acton, 2005. The author

However, the latter was stopped at a level crossing, which his quarry was just able to beat and continue his murderous trail. Luckily, Mrs Sell later recovered in Acton Hospital, though her arm had been shattered. She later recalled, 'Everything happened so suddenly.' Five minutes later, Winnifred Allenby was fired upon, but escaped injury. Another innocent bystander was Miss Hunt, formerly headmistress at Grange Infants' School, Ealing, who was shot at in West Ealing, but fortunately, the aiming was poor this time and she escaped unscathed. By now it had been an hour since the slaughter had begun.

He then drove in a north-westerly direction, reaching Bruton Way, Ealing, at about 10.10. He knocked on the door of one of the houses there. Its occupant, Mrs Edith Barringer, answered. She was about to speak to him, when he shot and killed her.

By now, the police were on his track. Police cars and motor cyclists were co-ordinated by radio and telephone and threw a net around London's western suburbs. Some officers were armed. He narrowly escaped being arrested in Harrow, but at noon, his car was spotted again, this time on Stanmore Broadway and the police gave chase. Finally, at the Watford bypass, a police car blocked the roundabout, and, after his car had been rammed, the man faced a muzzle of a rifle. Their quarry then surrendered and this strange drama was brought to a close. Constables Laver and Perceval were commended by their superintendent for showing 'great courage' when making the arrest. At 2.30 pm, the triple murderer was in Edgware Police Station and was then brought to Hammersmith.

So who was this man who had shot dead three people and wounded another three in less than 3 hours? The killer was Philip Joseph Ward, a 31-year-old soldier, who served in the Royal Artillery at Newmarket in an anti-aircraft battery. He was a 'thick-set man of more than medium height and thinning light brown hair'. Ward was charged with the murders at the inquest held in Brentford on 15 November. All the inquests were adjourned – that of Mrs Barringer to 29 November. Ward was charged with murder, and replied, 'Murder – that's a nasty word'. He denied everything. When questioned about the killing of Ludford, he said, 'Who is he? I don't know him. Do you? What are you charging me here for . . . I again say I am innocent and don't know him.' In court, Ward smiled at journalists, magistrates and policemen. He was remanded in custody for three weeks.

It was only now that the events leading up to the murder could be learnt. Although from a lower middle class background, Ward had been unemployed throughout the 1930s. In 1937, Ward, then known as Ross Brent, lived in Acton. There he had been a member of the Brentford and Chiswick Conservative Club. In the November of that year, his membership had been cancelled because he had been harassing one Barbara Savage, a female member of the club. She later recalled: 'His manner and talk were stupid.' On one occasion, they had been dancing and he said to her 'I would like to see you in a white bathing costume.' These advances were not reciprocated. He then sent her anonymous letters and telegrams, declaring 'I am holding a torch to you', which Barbara thought were silly rather than obscene.

Bruton Way, Ealing, 2005. The author

The chairman of the committee who had decided to ask him to cancel his membership was Leslie Ludford. The secretary of the same committee was Mrs Simmond. This dismissal enraged Ward, and a long and acrimonious correspondence ensued. Ludford was even assaulted during a game of whist because of it. The two were separated and Ward told Ludford, 'Just because you are a cripple, you think you can do as you like'. This was not the end of the quarrel, but the beginning of Ward's obsession with avenging himself on those he deemed had wronged him.

With the onset of the Second World War, Ward was called up for military service. In December 1940, Ward ordered a shotgun from J. Rigby and Co., of Sackwell Street, a London firm of gunmakers. It cost him £26 7s and arrived the following month. On 7 November 1941, he was granted a week's leave. On the following day he arrived at a guest-house in Barrowsgate Road, Chiswick, where he had stayed during his leave on previous occasions. He could then plot his revenge. A car, a Hillman saloon, number GGC 83, was hired from Queensbury Hire Services for 9–13 November at the price of £9 9s. He put his gun into a brown fibre suitcase and then drove to Hadley Gardens, arriving just before 9.00 in the morning.

As noted, there was a tenuous motive why Ward had shot Ludford and why he had shot the two women who were at Mrs Simmond's house. But why he shot at Mrs Sell or the others is unknown. Although Mrs Barringer's husband later told the court that his wife had had no connection with Ward whatsoever, Ward had belonged to the same tennis club in Hanwell as her adult children. It is possible that Ward made advances towards her daughter and when these were rejected, he blamed it on the mother's influence and decided to have his revenge. The other women who had been shot at had no discernible link with Ward whatsoever. But perhaps, by then, blood-lust predominated over even tenuously rational feelings. As a police-man noted 'The motive for this case cannot be given unless it is merely the lust to kill by WARD after having seen previous persons collapse as a result of his wanton shooting.' Yet the planning of the murders had been meticulous and cold-blooded enough. The full explanation behind the slayings was to emerge later.

On 26 December, Ward was formally committed for trial at the Old Bailey. He stated he intended to plead, 'Not Guilty'. Yet, for all the drama of his shooting spree, the finale was not a sensational court case in January 1942, but a damp squib. On 19 January, it was deemed that Ward was unfit to plead. Sir Gerald Dobson, Recorder of the City of London, stated that Ward would be detained at His Majesty's pleasure. He was suffering from schizophrenia and so would be unable to follow the course of any trial or properly instruct the counsel acting on his behalf. It also emerged that he had been certified insane as long ago as 1932, but, though he had not been considered to have been cured, he was discharged a year later, as he was a voluntary patient. However, he had passed his medical examinations on joining the Army in 1940, being classified as being both stable and Grade 1 in fitness.

In an interview with Dr Grierson at Brixton Prison in 1942, he revealed that he had a persecution complex. He had been a loner all his life and had been difficult at home. Ward confessed, 'It's a scandal the way people have treated me, perfect strangers and in strange parts ... They communicate with each other and have made me an outcast and spoilt my whole life.' He told the doctor his chilly resolution, 'I can't fight millions of people. Therefore, a few must suffer.' It was this form of insanity, together with his being frustrated four years previously, which made him take his deadly course. It is presumed that he was eventually sent to Broadmoor for life; all the files reveal is that he was 'detained during His Majesty's pleasure'.

At the time of writing, the full story cannot be told because Ward is still alive and, under the Data Protection Act of 1998, his full medical history cannot be viewed.

Chapter 28

Double Murder
1943

Mrs Brewer often screamed in fun when her husband was sparring with her.

The second double murder in Ealing during the Second World War came two years after the Crocker/Watson case. Again, a man killed a woman and her small child.

Readers of the *Middlesex County Times* were doubtless shocked to read in September 1943 that Mrs Gladys Lavina Brewer, aged 20, and her 2-year-old baby, Shirley, had been found dead with their heads smashed in, at 1 Grove Flats, Grove Place (demolished in the early 1980s to make way for the Ealing Broadway Shopping Centre). Mrs Brewer had been last seen alive on Wednesday, 8 September 1943. A scream had been heard at 11 o'clock that evening, but after that nothing more.

Mrs Elsie Sewell, a neighbour from the flat above, went around on the following day, as the blackout curtains had not been taken down, even though it was broad daylight. Taking a look inside, she decided to call the police. Forcing an entry, the officers found Mrs Brewer in a chair in the kitchen. There were signs of her having been beaten as well as having her head smashed. Around her neck was a note addressed to her husband, who was a petty officer serving in the Patrol Service of the Royal Navy. He was aged 22 and had been recently on leave, returning for duty on 1 September. Next door they made another frightful discovery – the body of her baby in her cot, killed in the same brutal manner as her mother.

Another neighbour, Mrs Blake, was able to shed some light on Mrs Brewer's last day alive. She said:

Mrs Brewer came into me with Shirley on Wednesday evening soon after the 6 o'clock news and smoked a cigarette. She appeared quite happy and normal and was laughing. Then she went indoors and put the baby to bed. She had two friends staying with her called Gladys and

Grove Place, Ealing. LBE

*Charlie and their baby boy. They came on Sunday and I saw them for
the first time on Wednesday evening about 7.30. I don't know their
surname, but I understand they were local people.*

Mrs Blake heard Mrs Brewer scream at 11.00 and shout, 'Don't
Ernie'. Then, the witness continued:

*I heard Shirley scream and something dropped on the floor which I took
to be the baby's bottle. I did not think anything of the incident at the
time as Mrs Brewer often screamed in fun when her husband was
sparring with her and Shirley always imitated her mother.*

Events moved quickly. On 10 September, Divisional Detective
William Tarr and Detective Inspector Norman saw Charles William
Koopman, aged 22, of the Royal Air Force, and his 21-year-old wife,
Gladys Patricia Koopman, of St Margaret's Road, Hanwell. They had
been detained by Slough Police for questioning in Ealing for the
murder of the Brewers. After having been cautioned at Ealing Police
Station, Koopman replied 'No' and his wife said nothing.

On the following day they were formally accused at Ealing Police
Court. Mrs Koopman seemed to be in a state of collapse, having to be
led from the cells by her husband and a wardress. During the hearing,
her head had to be held up and she sat in a chair. They were remanded
in custody until 21 September.

Meanwhile, the deputy coroner for West Middlesex, Dr Gorsky,
opened the inquest. A large crowd gathered outside the Brentford
Police Court at Half Acre, to see the principals – the latter including
Ernie Brewer, the widower, and Mrs Koopman. Edward Handsford,
Mrs Brewer's father, a Hanwell man and a member of the Ealing Civil
Defence corps, identified the corpses. He had last seen them alive on
2 September. Mrs Sewell told how she had found the bodies and
Inspector Tarr of how he had arrived on the scene at 3.15. On the day
after the inquest, a packed funeral took place at Ealing Cemetery.
There was much local sympathy for the family of the deceased.

The case against the Koopmans began at Ealing Police Court on
21 September with evidence from the neighbours. The more interesting revelation was the content of the letter which had been found
around the dead woman's neck. It had been written by Koopman and
began,

*Dear Ernie, I am sorry to do this to you, and please God forgive me, but
I am afraid your wife is very immoral. We are going the same way soon
and I hope just as quickly. We don't know you personally, but we know
your heart, and believe me, when you get over the shock, you will be
better off. God forgive us.*

It was unsigned. It is unlikely the widower would have agreed, as he stated that his wife was 'a good tempered girl, but she was rather outspoken'.

Koopman then explained himself, starting with the background to the murder. First, he said his wife had nothing to do with the killing and she was taken out of the court forthwith. Five years before, he had courted Gladys Handsford as she was then but they had only had three dates. He had been in love with her, but found 'she was of a loose type and made dates which she did not keep'. Once they were alone in her father's house, but she frightened him – by pulling him on top of her whilst on her father's bed with obvious intent – and he stopped seeing her. In 1941 he married his present wife. They were very happy together and had a son, Ronald. They initially lived in Hayes, before moving to live with Mrs Koopman's parents.

One day in September 1942, Koopman and his wife had been out shopping and chanced to see Mrs Brewer. He introduced his wife to his old flame, and, feeling lonely because of her husband's absence, Mrs Brewer suggested that they pay her a visit one evening. This they did on six occasions. Mrs Koopman allegedly disliked Mrs Brewer because the latter was said to have wanted to kiss her husband.

On 5 September, Mrs Koopman, miserable that her husband was about to return to active service, wanted to run away with him. They stayed with Mrs Brewer for a few days. On the evening of 7 September, the two went out to see a film at the Broadway Palladium, then went to three pubs, including the *Three Pigeons* (now the *Park View*) and the *Railway Hotel*, both on Ealing High Street, drinking beer and whisky. They then went to Mrs Brewer's at just after 10.00. Koopman was feeling a little drunk and teased his host by turning the gas up and down, whilst his wife said they should leave.

Koopman then said Mrs Brewer cried,

> *'Stop it!' I suppose that at that moment I thought of all the bad things against her and how immoral she was. I took a hammer with the intent to frighten her. I know I struck her on the head with a hammer. My wife said, 'Don't do it' and grabbed my arm to stop me. Then I heard the baby Shirley, crying. I took the torch into the bedroom and struck the child with the hammer repeatedly until she stopped crying.*

They then emptied Mrs Brewer's purse of money, took her rings and Koopman wrote a note, which concluded 'What I have done I would not have done in my right state of mind. It must have been the drink I had.' The Koopmans and their little son then left, at about midnight. They caught a train to Slough to try and find shelter with a friend, John Humphreys, who was told that they were looking for his aunt in Slough but could not find her. In any case, he was at first happy to accommodate them. Humphreys soon learnt that the Koopmans were sought by the police, but was concerned because Koopman had a loaded gun. He took Koopman to The Dog and Pot, a local pub, and they were confronted (as arranged) by the police. Asked if he was Koopman, he denied it and gave a false name. When Humphreys correctly named him, they were taken into police custody. Koopman later said that all he was concerned about was his wife, and took upon himself all the responsibility for the crimes. Mr Brewer identified the two rings as being his wife's and said the hammer (found under the baby's cot) was his and was usually housed in the coal cellar.

Koopman was committed for trial at the Old Bailey on 27 October. He pleaded not guilty. The case for the prosecution, directed by Anthony Hawke and Mr Elam, was that Koopman had killed his ex-girlfriend and her child with a hammer. The difficulty was with motive – although cash had been taken, that was not why Mrs Brewer had been slain. Therefore, Messrs Linton Thorpe and Shaw, for the defence, argued that Koopman was not in his right mind. At the police court hearing, Dr Teare, the pathologist at St George's Hospital, remarked that the blows which killed Mrs Brewer were consistent with those struck by someone who was not fully sane, but, equally, that they could have been caused by a man who was in full possession of his mental faculties.

It was put to Dr Teare that the vaccination Koopman had had against smallpox might have affected his mind, but the doctor said that that would only be the case in one in 100,000. He did not think it even remotely possible that the vaccination could have resulted in Koopman becoming a homicidal maniac. Other doctors were called in to give their opinions as to whether Koopman was insane and they varied in their view. Some said he was of a naturally aggressive tendency, having assaulted his mother and mother-in-law in the past, but what this proved was open to question. There was certainly no insanity in the family, though his father and his grandfather were also known to be bad tempered. Dr Hill claimed that,

We can find no evidence that his consciousness was impaired at the time, or evidence that he did not know what he was doing, or that he did not know that it was wrong.

Understandably, the jury was confused at so many possibilities. They spent 90 minutes in deliberation before asking the judge, Justice Asquith, for the definition of insanity as regards the law. They were told that a man was insane if he knew what he was doing, but did not know it was wrong. Ten minutes later, they returned a verdict of guilty. In passing the death sentence, Asquith commented that, if Koopman was insane, it was odd that he had been able to give such an ordered account of the case.

But that was not the end. There was an appeal, challenging the verdict, a month later. Although not doubting that Koopman was the killer, Thorp argued that the vaccination which Koopman had been administered had given him a rare disease of the mind. The medical evidence on this point, Thorp argued, had not been contradicted by the prosecution. He also pointed out that Koopman had not been told that he had the right to challenge the jury. The court believed these points were academic and dismissed the case. On 13 December, Dr Newsam wrote 'the Secretary of State has been unable to find any sufficient ground to justify him in advising His Majesty to interfere with the due course of law'. Therefore, Koopman was hanged at Pentonville Prison two days later.

Chapter 29

Husband and Wife 1952

I did it, guv, with this bayonet. She has been two-timing me.

After the Second World War, building proceeded rapidly in the north-western corner of Ealing, in the hitherto rural parish of Northolt. New houses and streets were everywhere by the early 1950s, fulfilling in part governmental promises to erect better housing for the working classes. Yet, for one young couple, their life here was short and violent.

Raymond Jack Cull, a 23-year-old labourer, first met Jean Frances Caton of Shadwell Drive in 1950. She was aged 14 or 15; her electro-plater father, Joseph, being uncertain of his daughter's age. Cull was an orphan. They then met each night if possible, but this happy state did not last long, especially after they rented rooms in Southall, and lived together. They often argued about the attention she received from other men.

The crisis came when Cull had to go into Isleworth Hospital for a kidney stone operation. It was just before they were to wed. When he came out after a fortnight, he was told that Jean had been seeing another man. She had met a man, who was married but separated from his wife, in Greenford and they had gone to a pub together. He was affluent, having a car and a flat. Yet, after a row, Cull and Jean were reconciled.

In March 1952 they were married and began living in Kenilworth Road, Ealing, but from then on, matters worsened. Their short married life was described in court as being 'troubled, full of rows and arguments, right from the beginning, partly through money and partly through jealousy on his part as she was not behaving as she should have done'. After one argument, a policeman called at the house and Jean told him that Cull had hit her and threatened her with a dagger, both of which Cull denied. The constable left after 'giving some fatherly advice'. Jean had said, 'my husband is trying to stop me going back to my mother; I refuse to stay with him', to which he answered,

'She has left me before and then come back. I don't want her to go.' According to her mother, he had also threatened to kill her, saying, 'She won't get out of here alive.'

But this was only a temporary lull in hostilities. Cull thought that his wife was forever trying to avoid him and he objected to her being with her mother, who, he thought, was a bad influence. They rowed and parted; she to her mother, he to his sister's. Soon afterwards, the tide seemed to have turned. Jean bought two tickets for a boxing match and asked her husband to accompany her. When he arrived at her mother's house, he was told that her brother Derek would go with her instead. Cull watched the fight on the television at her father's house and then waited for his wife to return. Derek appeared without Jean and Cull became suspicious, especially as Derek was vague about his sister's movements.

A motorcyclist arrived with Jean in tow at 1.00 in the morning. Harsh words were exchanged when the motorcyclist departed and then Cull held his wife around the throat, demanding to be told where the man lived. The frightened girl refused to say and the pressure on her throat was released. Cull profusely apologised to her the next day and told her that he only meant to frighten her, rather than to do her any real harm. Not everyone agreed on that point and a court order

Shadwell Drive, Northolt, 2005. The author

Thorne Way, Northolt, 2005. The author

was sent to him soon afterwards, asking him to attend the court, but he did not do so.

The two were together again for a brief spell, but trouble was never far away. Her father warned him to stay away. Cull told his wife that he did not want her to see other men.

Jean eventually went back to live with her father and her two younger sisters at Shadwell Drive, while Cull lived at the nearby Thorne Close. This resulted in another argument between the two of them. Cull made threats to kill her on more than one occasion. He also wrote love letters to her, pleading with her to return to him or he would kill her. One was addressed 'My loving wife, Jeannie' and another 'Beloved Sweetheart'. One of the letters read:

> *I am heart-broken because you won't see me. I am sorry for what has happened and I pray for the Lord's forgiveness and yours . . . After you left me I had nothing left. My darling I am crying as I write this letter. I am going to bed but without food or water and I will stay there until you come and see me. If you don't come I will will myself to die because I cannot live without you. And if you don't I am sending you my last kiss before I pass away. From your broken-hearted husband, Johnny.*

Cull was clearly desperate, but no one else saw the danger signs. Matters began to reach a climax. On Saturday morning of 28 June, Cull waited outside her father's address for her to return home. At 2.30 a taxi drew up and his wife got out. The other passenger, a man, remained and the car drove off. Questioned as to who the man was, Jean eventually said he was the brother of a girl friend of hers. They had been at her friend's house, playing cards, before going out to the cinema. Jean said that she did these things 'to prove to herself whether she could go out with another man and still enjoy herself'. This might have annoyed Cull, but her next words were conciliatory. She was not going to see much of her mother any more and would live with him again.

They went indoors and slept together. Cull later said, 'I thought she really meant what she said and I was very happy.' Although he left a few hours later, she told him to give her a call in the afternoon. Coming home from work, he found a letter addressed to him. The note stated her mind quite plainly. 'I don't want you any more. Please understand I just don't want to see you any more. I cannot love you any more ... Jeannie, Goodbye.'

It had a devastating impact. Cull tried to forget her but without success. He went out and drank beer, becoming intoxicated in the process. By the evening, though, he was not drunk. He went home and then decided to try and see her again. He took a fourteen-inch bayonet with him in case her father tried to prevent him seeing her, though it was only intended to frighten.

Cull climbed into the house by the back window, which was open on that summer night. Removing his shoes, he quietly entered her bedroom. He tried to awaken her quietly, and succeeded. It was then that the tragedy occurred. According to Cull, his wife tried to wrest the weapon from him, but fell onto him and it. He claimed he did not recall thrusting it into her body. One thing is clear, however; Jean was stabbed in the chest and the resulting haemorrhage killed her.

Her scream woke up her father who was in the adjacent bedroom. Opening the door to investigate and wearing only his underclothes, he saw Cull, bayonet in hand, standing over the motionless body of his eldest daughter, his hands wet with blood. It was a picture of startling horror. Caton began to shout and then fled, pursued by Cull. The former escaped, running down Shadwell Drive and then into Court Mead Road and the latter returned to the scene of the crime. He tried to lift his victim up and to get help, but was unable to do so as the effects of the alcohol drunk earlier had not yet worn off. His wife was not quite dead and began to moan incoherently. Cull tried to talk to her, but to no avail.

Cull then decided to summon official help. Walking to a nearby shop, he smashed the window and used the telephone inside to dial 999. By now there were people milling about in the street and he was convinced they were watching him. He then went to his sister's house, which was nearby. He confessed all to her, sobbing, 'I think I have killed Jeannie.' It was here where the police arrested him. He made no attempt to flee from the police or to evade responsibility, telling them that, 'I did it, guv, with this bayonet. She has been two-timing me ...

She asked for it. I will take what is coming to me.' He was full of remorse however, and a doctor who later examined him remarked, 'He says he is very sorry that his wife is dead and that he was very much in love with her. I think his expression of remorse is genuine.'

Chief Detective Inspector Robert Richardson was in charge of the case and he first confronted Cull at 12.45 on Sunday morning at Greenford Police Station. He told Cull, 'I am a police officer. I have just been to Shadwell Drive, Greenford, and I have seen the dead body of your wife. You will be detained pending enquiries.' Cull gave a cool reply, 'That's ok, sir.' Richardson continued, 'Do you wish to make any statement?' to which the answer was, 'I am upset just now. I will have a sleep and tell you what happened later.'

The inquest was held on 1 July. Caton provided the necessary identification. The pathologist, Mr Teare stated the cause of death and then the inquest was adjourned until 30 September. This was because 'in as much as a man has been charged with the murder of Mrs Cull, the law provides that the inquest shall not proceed but must be adjourned until after the criminal proceedings have been concluded'.

On 30 June, Cull made a two-minute appearance in the dock at Ealing Magistrates' Court to be charged with murder. Richardson asked that Cull be held on remand for another week, on account of the evidence against him. This was granted. Then Mr Scholfield, the clerk of the court, asked Cull if he desired legal aid. After a moment's thought, Cull agreed. His voice was barely audible. Mr Garrod, the chairman of the court, told him that this would be granted.

There was another request for a remand made in the following week by Detective Inspector Harris as he said the prosecution was not ready to proceed yet. Mr Hall, who had been chosen to act on Cull's behalf, raised no objection to this, but said, 'I would like to know the date when the prosecution would be ready.' Harris replied by saying, 'The most I can say is that we hope to start the case next week, but I cannot be definite.' Hall asked if Cull's brother-in-law could visit him and this was granted.

After the hearing at the magistrates' court, in which Cull pleaded not guilty, he was sent down for trial. There was a psychiatric and medical examination to learn more about Cull. It seemed he was the youngest of ten children, had been a slow developer and had been sent to an approved school at the age of 12. He then began working in a garage at 14. His national service in the Army had been satisfactory. He had been a heavy drinker since 18. There was no mental illness in the family, and whilst of below average intelligence, he was not feeble minded. It was concluded that he had had 'a poor early home environment and a poor work record'.

On 12 September, the case was heard at the Old Bailey. The prosecution led by Mr Christmas Humphreys QC, stated that, because his wife wished to leave him, Cull had killed her with a bayonet, though the defence said that her death was an accident, and that she had fallen on the weapon as her husband held it. Mr John Maude QC, defending, demonstrated that this was possible by pushing the bayonet against his junior colleague, Mr Hemming. The jury found Cull guilty of murder and added a rider that he should be recommended for mercy. When pronouncing the death sentence, Mr Justice Donovan said that he would pass on this recommendation. However, this was to no avail. On 30 September, Cull was hanged at Pentonville Prison.

There is no doubt that this tragedy was one of two people marrying too young and with completely different emotional and social needs. They reacted together like angry chemicals in the same test tube until at last the whole blew up, destroying each one. A sad waste of two young lives.

Chapter 30

'Portrait of a Very Bad Man' 1954

When you receive this letter I won't be alive any more. I am innocent.

The final chapter of murder in Ealing in the period under review is one of its most notorious. It is also the only one in which the murder was carefully planned and executed, and for which the murderer constructed an apparently unbreakable alibi. This device is beloved of novelists of the 'Golden Age of Crime Fiction', but is rare in reality.

For Eileen Thorpe, the 18-year-old housemaid, Thursday 11 February 1954, began like any other day, reporting to her place of work, a privately run old people's home in Montpelier Road, Ealing. The establishment was run by a mother and daughter partnership from about 1949. The mother was 'Lady' Mary Menzies, aged 73. Her daughter was Mrs Veronica Chesney, aged 43 and wife of Lieutenant Commander Ronald John Chesney, whom she had married in 1928. Miss Thorpe began her duties, which, as usual, included bringing tea up to her employers. It was odd that she could not find either of them. When an ambulance arrived later that morning, with another patient, she let them in herself. They found that the bathroom door was locked and the back door was open, but could find nothing else which was suspicious. It was only in the afternoon that the bathroom key was produced and then turned in the lock and a grisly discovery was made.

The police were called, arriving at 2.45 pm. Mrs Chesney's corpse was found in the bathroom, and a search of the house of death found the concealed body of her mother. The initial statement issued by Scotland Yard was 'Death in both cases may have been caused by manual stangulation.'

Chief Superintendent Thomas Barrett of Scotland Yard led the enquiries and the medical examinations were conducted by Dr Teare of the Home Office. The body of Mrs Chesney had been found in a state of semi-undress in the bathroom, while that of her mother was found in a disused lounge at the back of the house, and her head had

Montpelier Road, Ealing. LBE

been battered. The house was searched and door-to-door enquiries were made in the neighbourhood. Meanwhile, the elderly residents were moved to other homes in Middlesex. However, a couple of them volunteered statements. Mrs Eccles had heard noises in the night and wondered if that had been Mrs Chesney returning from a night out. Another resident, Mrs Jell, recalled that Mary Menzies had said goodnight to her.

The police investigation extended to other parts of Ealing and London. They found out from the neighbours that Lady Menzies owned property elsewhere and that there were three grandchildren who also helped out at the home. Plaster casts were made of tyre and footprints near to the house. A number of objects were removed from the house – a large white bust, a clock and a table lamp – for further examination. It was also confirmed that 'Lady' Menzies had no right to her title, which she had assumed on marrying her second husband in 1930. The line had died out in 1911. Meanwhile a manhunt began. Descriptions of a man – as yet unidentified by name – were being circulated. It was stated that he might have recently left the country. Ports were checked. He was described as being 'of middle age and has a beard. It is also thought he may be wearing gold ear-rings.' A man fitting this description had been seen by neighbours in recent times.

One neighbour said she saw 'a middle aged man walking up and down Montpelier Road after having been refused admittance to the home'. Who was he? The murderer?

The next key development in the case was the discovery by a postal worker of Ronald Chesney's body in a clearing in a wood near Cologne, on 16 February. He had been shot through the head and an American colt revolver lay by his side. On his body was a passport in the name of John Donald Miller. When the German police contacted Scotland Yard, officers flew to Cologne to investigate.

It was then that Chesney's past life began to be examined and a colourful one it was (for simplicity's sake he shall be referred to Chesney throughout). He had been born in 1907 as John Donald Merrett, into an affluent background, though his father died when he was a child. As an 18-year-old undergraduate, he attended Edinburgh University. But his allowance was insufficient to meet the needs of the lifestyle he aspired to. In order to afford high living he turned to forging his mother's signature to obtain money by cashing cheques allegedly in her name. Eventually, alerted by her banker, she realized that her only child was stealing from her. Chesney then used the revolver which he had purchased to impress a girlfriend and killed his mother. Initially it was assumed to be suicide, but Chesney was tried for her murder. Luckily for him, Spilsbury spoke for the defence and told the jury that the dead woman's injuries could have been self-inflicted. After an eight-day trial, the fifteen-strong jury returned a verdict of not proven. Chesney was convicted on the lesser charge of forging cheques to the value of £457 and was given a year in prison. On leaving prison, he took the name of Milner and then that of Chesney.

Chesney married Veronica Menzies after being befriended by 'Lady' Menzies, a friend of his mother's, who believed in his innocence. Chesney settled on his wife the sum of £8,400; but she could only touch the interest. On her death, the capital would revert to him. Conventional domestic life did not suit Chesney, however, and for much of the 1930s, he and his wife were in or around the Mediterranean. Chesney had decided to assume the role of the sailor and bought a fast yacht.

The yacht was not just for pleasure or as a mere symbol. It was to be used for profit and to keep Chesney in money without the bane of any real work. Not legitimate work, that was. He became a smuggler and would ferry anything for anyone if it paid. In the prelude to the Spanish Civil War, he ran consignments of guns to the eventual insurgents. Chesney became a well-known figure in the disreputable criminal underworld. This, together with his drinking, womanizing and gambling rapidly estranged his wife.

However, the pair returned to England at the outbreak of war in 1939 and they settled in St Mary's Road, Ealing. Before Chesney was called up, he and his wife drove ambulances for the local civil defence service. At the outset of the following year, Chesney's real war service began and he was enrolled in the Royal Navy Volunteer Reserve. His experience with boats enabled him to obtain the rank of Lieutenant Commander and his colleagues soon learnt he was a show off and a braggart. Yet he also possessed a flashy kind of bravery. In 1942 he led gunboats to help the beleaguered garrison of Tobruk, and at its fall in 1942, his boat sinking, Chesney continued to fire his gun in defiance before being captured. He escaped from the Italians, but was later recaptured and in 1943 was repatriated to England.

Chesney saw little more active service, but he did join the army of occupation of Germany in 1945. This enabled him to smuggle and loot the defeated nation of anything he could lay his hands on. Apart from self-aggrandisement, he also met one Gerda Schalla, a young German refugee from the East. She fell in love with this seemingly dashing rogue and the two travelled around Europe and the Mediterranean from 1946 to 1950. He and his wife were now living completely separate lives.

In this period, Chesney returned to his old game of smuggling. This brought rewards, but also setbacks. He was convicted on a number of occasions for forging cheques, obtaining goods by false pretences, theft in Hamburg, trafficking in currency in Paris, using false names and other crimes. In 1951, he spent a year in an English prison. It was at this time that Gerda, tired of his criminal and adulterous ways, left him. Sonia Winnicke became his next mistress. We shall return to Chesney in a moment.

When the British police arrived at Cologne they conferred with their German counterparts and searched Chesney's possessions. They also spoke to Sonia. She told them that she received a note from her late lover. It read, 'After all that lies behind me, I have no chance, and as I have not seen one tonight I am ending everything. When you receive this letter I won't be alive any more. I am innocent.' Sonia told the police that Chesney had told her a few days before that he was planning to return to England, after he had read about the murders.

Local opinion also thought Chesney innocent, too. The local newspaper stated:

There was no evidence to connect Chesney with the murders, nor was
there anything to show that he was in the country when the crimes were

committed. Chesney is known to have been in England at the end of last month but to have left via Harwich on 4 February.

Chesney was a well-known figure who flitted in and out of Ealing. His appearance made him memorable – he was usually accompanied by a boxer dog and his gold ear-ring made him stand out, though he spoke but little.

The police took the view that the murders had been well planned. They thought that the killing of Mrs Chesney was set up to look like an accident. She had been drinking and the killer had made it look as if she drowned while drunk in her bath. However, the plan then went awry as Lady Menzies heard noises from the bathroom and went to investigate. She was hit on the side of the head, strangled and then the body was hidden in a little used room.

Had Chesney committed the crime and then decided, once the police were on his track, to end it all, rather than face trial for murder? He may have feared that his criminal past would have been held against him in court and so the outcome – hanging by the neck – would have been a foregone conclusion. Yet a suspect is only tried on the one charge and his past is not disclosed.

The inquest was held at Ealing Town Hall on 23–24 March. The public gallery was packed and hundreds crowded outside, mostly women. Evidence was brought forward to show, beyond any reasonable doubt, the truth of what really happened at Montpelier Road on the night of 10 February and why. The accumulation of evidence was difficult to argue with.

First of all, there were the letters which were found in the house, all addressed to Mrs Chesney, from her husband. The main thrust of them was similar. The following extract was read out in court:

I don't think we have anything much more to discuss about divorce. I know where I stand if you don't change your mind. I hope we shall be able to get cracking soon. It will be better for both of us.

Miss McNeish, an adopted daughter of Mrs Chesney, said that Chesney wanted a divorce so he could marry Gerda, and then when that broke up, Sonia. But his wife refused because she was a Catholic and, furthermore, did not want to let a German woman have a British passport. Miss McNeish added, 'Latterly, I have heard Mrs Chesney say that her husband had said she was worth more dead than alive to him.'

Secondly, several witnesses came forward who said that Chesney had offered them money to kill his wife. Richard Pickersgill had shared a cell in Pentonville with Chesney. He offered Pickersgill

£2,000 to commit the murder. Pickersgill said: 'Chesney also said he would try to get me a gun but at the time could not get one. I told Chesney that I would not agree to any of these arrangements.' Another ex-prisoner, Herbert Boyd, said:

> *He told me he wanted to get rid of his wife so that he could have the money that was in a marriage settlement and marry Sonia ... He offered me £1,000 to run down Mrs Chesney with a car.*

Then there was the physical evidence. On Mrs Chesney's cardigan was one of Chesney's hairs. Under Chesney's fingernails were woollen fibres which matched his wife's cardigan. Chesney's hairs were found on Lady Menzies's slippers. Chesney's cardigan concealed a tuft of his wife's headscarf. His clothing also had dog hairs that matched those of the two dogs in the house. No one had heard the dogs bark on the night of the murder as they would have if a stranger had entered. But Chesney was on friendly terms with the dogs (as with the famous Sherlock Holmes tag, it was what man's best friend did not do which was significant). There were also scratch marks on his hands and wrists which were only a few days old and consistent with those inflicted by someone fighting to avoid being strangled.

Finally, there was a positive identification. Miss Patricia Marsh, who lived nearby, recalled that she had been taking her dog for a walk on the evening of 10 February. She saw a man who 'gave me rather a fright ... He was tall, heavily built and was walking with a limp. There was a lamp on the other side of the road and I saw his face clearly.' When shown a picture of Chesney, she said that the two were identical. Another neighbour, Peter Henderson, also saw Chesney on that night.

The circumstantial evidence against Chesney was very strong. He had motive, but he also had an alibi. That was easily broken. He had used another man's passport to re-enter the country just a few days after he had left it. Airport staff and other witnesses recognized him as having made a journey by Dutch airways on 11 February. It was also discovered how he had entered the house, without a key but not having to break in. He had recently visited the house on 4 February, where he had set in motion his plans for re-entry unnoticed. All he had to do was to approach the house at the rear, and to remove a stone and a wooden screw in order to gain access to the house by the French windows.

Chesney was found guilty of the double murder. As with the case in 1927, he had been able to cheat the hangman again, but this time, at least, it was for the last time.

Conclusion

number of murders took place in Ealing from the late sixteenth century to the mid-1950s. At least forty-nine to be exact, not counting a number of infanticides; though not all these crimes are chronicled here, due to lack of space. This is a very small number. Far more people died of accidents, illness and old age. For example, in 1935 alone, a dozen people died in road accidents in Greenford. Ealing and its environs were far from being a dangerous place as far as murder was concerned. A true picture can only be made when there is comparative data from other districts, so this tentative conclusion will have to suffice until then. Certainly, compared to more recent years, the murder rate was low and compares favourably to that of 1972–87, when thirty-nine people were murdered in the borough (or the dozen murders which occurred between September 2004 and October 2005). Arguably the population in more recent times has been higher than it was until at any point until the early twentieth century, but the point still holds: Ealing's murder rate was historically low. A further point is that, until at least 1954, murders appeared as front page headlines; something which is no longer guaranteed.

But what of the murders themselves? All twenty-eight discussed here were committed by men, except for the infanticides. There were three double murders and one triple murderer. Their victims were fourteen women, ten men and four children. The methods of murder were as follows: eight shootings, nine stabbings or slashings, two strangulations, six bludgeonings, two poisonings and an axe murder. Motives were mixed. In only four did money play a part, and eleven are unknown. Six were due to insanity and one depression. Six were due to frustrated love, overprotectiveness and fear a loved one would leave. Of the twenty-eight killings, only four were unsolved. In most cases, the killer turned out to be someone well known to the victim and was the most obvious suspect. The detection involved was not that of the fictional sleuth in the classic whodunnit, but more a case of proving that the suspect was guilty in order to satisfy a jury. None of the killers seem to have been particularly clever, as some noted murderers have been, though those who got away with it were undoubtedly lucky. Murderers and their victims came from all ranks of society; starting at the top with the likes of Perceval and Terriss, to the middle class world of the Chesneys and of Derrick and Wheeler, then descending to the working class milieu of the Deanes and the Fieldings.

The sentences doled out to the twenty-three guilty men varied. Seven were hanged, three were given prison sentences and three were deemed insane and sent to Broadmoor. Four cheated the hangman by committing suicide. Four were undetected, and one escaped. Only one was acquitted. For those who oppose capital punishment, little comfort can be found in this book, for all those sentenced to death were undoubtedly guilty of murder. As noted, in cases where the suspect did kill his victim, if extenuating circumstances could be found, as in the case of Derrick, the charge became one of manslaughter and not murder, or he was reprieved, in the case of Deane.

Cases of murder invoke sympathy for the victim and, occasionally, the guilty. Perhaps the most terrible cases were the murder and assault of Ada Shepherd in 1880, and the double murder of the Brewers in their home in 1943. Deane is the killer who gained most public sympathy. Ealing may still be regarded, at least historically, as 'Queen of the Suburbs', but it must be recalled that there was a serpent even in Eden.

Appendix

Other Murders Known to have been committed in and around Ealing (1692–1954)

1693: Henry Lambe was killed in Acton and Nicholas Charlton was found not guilty.

1755: Abraham Moore was killed in Ealing by Richard Matthews and was branded.

1760: Elizabeth Odell was killed in Ealing by her husband, William, who was hanged.

1763: Mr Rooker was killed in Ealing by person or persons unknown.

1823: Samuel Dance was killed in Ealing and John Hill, William Wadsworth and William Blagrave were found guilty of manslaughter.

1829: John Dwyer was killed in Ealing and Daniel Reading was found not guilty.

1853: Richard Medhurst was killed by person or persons unknown in East Acton.

1893: Annie Moorby, aged 7, was killed in Ealing by Benjamin Scotcher, who committed suicide.

1910: Annie Covell was killed in Ealing by her lover, Alfred Perry, who was hanged.

1915: Gladys Ruxton was killed in Ealing by her husband, John, who committed suicide.

1930: George Gerrard was killed by Abraham Cohen, a fellow inmate at St Bernard's Hospital.

1940: Leslie Wilkesman was killed in Perivale by Dudley Stone, who was insane.

1940: Pauline Wiltshire was gassed by her father, George, in Southall, who committed suicide.

1945: Linda Thorpe was killed in Hanwell by her mother, Doris, who was gaoled for two years.

1946: Marjorie Thompson was killed in Southall by her husband, Victor, who was hanged.

1947: Inga Peterson was killed in Ealing by person or persons unknown.

1950: Jean Brealing was killed in Greenford by her mother, who committed suicide.

1951: Sarah Farley was killed in Northolt by her husband, Maurice, who committed suicide.

1952: Andrzej Stopyra, was killed by Stanislaus Stopyra, a fellow inmate at St Bernard's Hospital.

1954: Victor Shadrake was killed in Acton by his father, Charles, who was insane.

1954: Mary Abery was killed in Acton by her husband, Henry, who committed suicide.

And there may be others.

Sources

Except those starred (*), all are available for consultation at Ealing Central Library – the others are available at the British Library or the National Archives.

Primary Sources – National Archives
Metropolitan Police
  Murder and Manslaughter files:* MEPO 3/1674, 1715, 1728, 2186, 2190, 2200 (part), 2260, 9452; CRIM1/1366, 2551
  Murder Registers:* MEPO 20/1–5

Primary Sources – Published Sources
Calendar of Close Rolls, IV, 1443–1447.*
Foxe, G *Acts and Monuments*, VII, 4th edn, 1583.
Calendar of the Middlesex Sessions
www.oldbaileyonline
The General Advertiser, 1747.*
The Annual Register, 1774, 1777, 1812.
The Morning Chronicle, 1777.*
The Gentleman's Magazine, 1777, 1812.
The Times, 1825, 1863, 1897–98, 1917.
The Buckinghamshire Advertiser, 1863.
The Acton Gazette, 1880, 1897, 1899, 1909, 1917, 1941-2.
The Southall-Norwood Gazette, 1895.
The Middlesex County Times, 1895, 1912, 1936, 1932, 1941, 1943, 1952, 1954.
The Acton Press, 1899.
The West Middlesex Gazette, 1938.
Lewis, W S (ed.) *Horace Walpole's Correspondence*, 1954.*
Tullett, T *A Portrait of a Bad Man*, 1956.
Boswell, J *Life of Johnson*, 1998.
Census Returns
Directories
Local Guides

Secondary Sources
Emsley, C *The English Police* (1991).
Fido, M *Murder Guide to London* (1988).
Gillens, M *The Assassination of the Prime Minister* (1972).

Hounsell, P *Ealing and Hanwell Past* (1991).
Lane, B *The Murder Club Guide to London* (1986).
Oates, J *Acton: A History* 2003).
Oxford Dictionary of National Biography (2004).
Spencer Shew, E *A Companion to Murder* (1960).
Spencer Shew, E *A Second Companion to Murder* (1961).

Index